About the Author

Jim Hay was born into a family of keen gardeners. After studying Engineering at the University of Strathclyde he worked in engineering design and is currently a senior glass-making technologist in the glass industry. In 1977, ill health forced him and his family to ban chemicals from their diet and he turned to organic gardening, concentrating on developing techniques for intensive cultivation in small growing areas. He now lectures widely on healthy living and is a member of the *Here's Health* gardening team.

Vegetables Naturally
ORGANIC GROWING FOR SMALL GARDENS

JIM HAY

Foreword by Jack Temple of *Here's Health*

CENTURY ARROW
London   Melbourne   Auckland   Johannesburg

A Century Arrow Book
Published by Arrow Books Limited
62–65 Chandos Place, London WC2N 4NW

An imprint of Century Hutchinson Ltd

London Melbourne Sydney Auckland
Johannesburg and agencies throughout
the world

First published 1985

Century Arrow edition 1986

Printed and bound in Great Britain by
The Guernsey Press Co. Ltd, Guernsey, C.I.

ISBN 0 09 946840 9

Contents

Foreword

by Jack Temple
Gardening Correspondent for *Here's Health* magazine

In writing the foreword to this book I want to stress that the object of organic cultivation is to improve the health and fertility of the soil, for only by doing so can the crops which are grown in this ground contain all the minerals and vitamins which are essential for a healthy life. Work at agricultural and horticultural research stations is showing that the chemicals so freely used in our modern methods of growing are causing an imbalance, locking up in the soil the vital minerals which therefore become lost to us. The soil which grows our food must be free of these chemicals to enable our food to give us the health we are entitled to.

Jim Hay, for the sake of his family's health, decided to convert to organic cultivation. However, seven or eight years ago the number of books available that really helped a chemical gardener to become an organic gardener were few and far between, particularly those containing concrete information on how to till tiny plots of land. That meant Jim had to learn the hard way.

I first met him on one of the gardening courses run by *Here's Health* magazine, by which time he had been following my articles in the magazine. He had weathered the disasters of the first year and was beginning to see some reward for his efforts, and by the end of the course was full of confidence he was on the right road. He knew that his new approach to gardening would pay off. Eventually the pests lessened and the favourable signs were beginning to indicate that the fertility and health of his soil had increased.

The rather limited area that Jim called his organic garden really meant that had he continued to garden in the traditional way he would hardly have been able to feed a sparrow, let alone his family. But Jim was persistent, very intuitive and dedicated. He has achieved an almost unheard-of state of self-sufficiency on land not much bigger than a postage stamp.

This book is a testament to the success of a tenacious approach to his growing problems. He developed the concept of making newspaper pots into a potential for giving prolonged greenhouse shelter to his growing plants simply by potting them on in larger home-made pots. There was no need, after this, to set plants outside in what one would normally call 'a very cold spot'. The chapter dealing with this method is so detailed that it would be almost impossible not to succeed when Jim's notes are followed.

This wealth of information is reflected in each chapter. Jim has always remembered his own struggles and his ignorance of the nitty gritty small details, which are vital if one has to turn failure into success. His meticulous attention to detail is of immense value to everyone interested in organic gardening on a small scale. Every crop included is covered with a step-by-step approach from the time the seed is sown until the time the vegetable has been cut and brought to the table.

In all my experience of growing I cannot remember picking up such a knowledgeable book, with masses of hints and tips which are normally ignored by the professional writer who mistakenly believes that these are known to all people. Jim knows better than that. Nobody reading this book will fail if they want to garden successfully enough to produce top-quality vegetables which are completely free from the smallest taint of poisons or chemicals – on any size plot! After all, where health is concerned we really must have food we can trust.

Jack Temple

Introduction

'You are what you eat.' I had always believed we ate very well with a freezer full of meat, vegetables and convenience foods, but the real meaning of the phrase was brought home in 1977 when ill health in the family forced a reassessment of our diet and its effect upon our lives. The end result was a conversion to wholefood vegetarianism.

It was easy to change from the supermarket over to the Health Food shop for most of the shopping, and for any item not available there a quick look at the ingredients for the dreaded preservatives and artificial colourings soon identified the non-acceptable. However, vegetables were to play an even more important role in our diet and where could we find a supply of chemically free, organically grown produce? There were several sources within about a 50-mile radius, but this would mean bulk buying and a lengthy trip every week as well as the loss of freshness of the produce towards the end of the week. There was nothing for it but to produce as much as possible from my own small garden, only 12 by 7.5 m (40 by 25 ft) in size.

Where does one start? My wife had picked up a copy of *Here's Health* magazine on one of her shopping trips and Jack Temple's articles were a boon in getting the project off the ground. Even so, with no compost and a chemical soil, the soil fertility during the first year was at a very low level and I suffered the consequences – a garden riddled with pests and, to make matters worse, I had to contend with disease imported the previous year when I had bought cabbage plants instead of growing my own.

I found relatives and friends of little help; they always appeared to have a convincing argument against organic growing at the times when my spirits and enthusiasm were at their lowest. I presume it is only human nature to be suspicious of someone who wanted to be different – it is only when you yourself are different that you can appreciate other points of view.

I was also being looked upon as a 'crank' with my distribution of polythene bags amongst the neighbours for their grass cuttings and kitchen waste, as well as the collecting of weeds (nettles and comfrey) from the surrounding waste land. In the end I decided to humour my critics and when asked why I was burying newspapers (for mulching) I would reply 'in the hope the potatoes will come up as chips' – I'm sure everyone knows we wholefooders do not eat chips!

The most difficult decision was how much land to allocate to compost making. I had read that compost would pay for itself ten times over, so I allocated ten per cent of my area. There was still a tendency to look at this amount and think how much more I could grow if I cropped it. However, the saying is perfectly true and the return more than compensates for the loss of growing space.

I survived that first disastrous year and from then on as the fertility levels rose the output from the garden never failed to amaze me, in quality and quantity. Any surplus went in the freezer and so my efforts to become self-sufficient on my 90 sq m (108 sq yd) had begun.

When giving talks about my growing methods, I am frequently confronted with the phrase 'my garden is too small'. I believe this impression arises from the message in books, magazines and television programmes that you need to be large to be successful, particularly when being advised on spacing – 1 m (3 ft) between rows, 60 cm (24 in) between plants, – the owner of a small garden cannot afford such luxury. It is true that life is easier on the larger scale: there is scope to grow a greater number of varieties and more of them and to stay with conventional growing methods. But the basic principles of compost making and mulching still apply and greater effort is needed to cover the larger area. The small garden, on the other hand, requires close attention to planning, particularly crop rotation, intercropping and successional cropping and the development of methods to squeeze a quart out of a pint pot. It is with the latter objective that my efforts have been channelled over recent years, devising ways of intensifying cropping to gain maximum output from a small garden. Soil fertility plays a very important role in my plans, for unless a high level is maintained, the soil is unable to support the large quantities I crop each year. Hence the emphasis on this subject in the early chapters.

Do not dismiss the large grower, however, for he has much to offer and we still have much to learn. It is surprising how often his methods apply to or can be adapted for the small garden.

I firmly believe that no garden, be it only a window-sill, is too small to grow a range of plants, even if only a small amount of each, which will supply organic produce for your household.

Once having dispensed with the chemicals and poisons, an awareness of the ecological aspects of these products very quickly develops. The organic garden is full of natural activity, each playing a role in producing a balance between the pest, its predators and yourself. Your attitude begins to alter towards the modern trend to kill off everything. There is plenty for all. What does it matter if the slug or caterpillar eats a few outer leaves? You were not going to eat them anyway. The slug and caterpillar is the basic diet of other animals, so why deprive them of their source of food? If you are forced into taking action, deter the pest or protect the plant; it is so much easier and safer.

Chapter One

Why grow organically?

What do we mean when we say we are going to grow organically? The dictionary defines the term as the production of food without the use of artificial fertilisers and pesticides. Although the concept is generations old the term 'organic gardening' was only introduced about 40 years ago. I feel a more apt expression would have been natural gardening, for that is what we are doing, reverting to the ways of nature. Not that we will end up with a wilderness of weeds – just the opposite. We'll have a garden of thriving plants, giving all the lifeforce, vitamins and minerals so necessary for a healthy body. We are going to work with nature, not against her, and where the habits of nature are a little slow for our needs, then we will give her all the assistance we can. To do this we must dispense with chemicals and use only products 'manufactured' by nature.

Why are we against the artificial products? After all, we live in an era of high technology, so why not take full advantage of all man's achievements? The argument falls into three categories: cost, ecology and health.

The cost factor is of little account for the amateur gardener, for many of the organic products available can be just as expensive as the chemical counterpart. For the commercial grower organic cultivation is very labour intensive, resulting in a cost which must be passed on to the purchaser.

It is a proven fact that the yield from chemical cultivation diminishes each year, and to compensate for this the rate of application needs to be increased, so the costs are rising each year. However, the arguments are not conclusive.

Chemical products can be subdivided into pesticides and fertilisers, so let us look at each in turn.

Pesticides

The argument against pesticides – and here we can include

herbicides – is fairly straightforward and familiar to most of us.

Anyone who has read *Silent Spring* by Rachel Carson will need no more convincing of the damage being done by the widespread use of these poisons, of how we are slowly, but surely, destroying ourselves and the environment by a desire to produce so-called better crops and more of them, and in doing so showing a total disregard for life. We are part of a chain and the interference in its balance will eventually catch up with us. Not only do these pesticides and herbicides have a disastrous effect on the plant, insect and animal life, but they also greatly affect us all.

Let us look at the two aspects of what actually occurs when these poisons are used. First of all, do we achieve our aims? Superficially, it is true the pest is killed off, but unfortunately poisons are not selective, so all insect life which comes in contact is affected, the good along with the bad. However, partly due to the sheer numbers and the fact that the lower forms of life are less susceptible to toxins in their environment, some of the pests escape to breed again, this time introducing immunity to the poison into the offspring. So the cycle is repeated and in some cases, as with aphids who can breed every 50 hours, the pest becomes resistant to the poison in one season.

Such is the extent of the speed in which immunity can be built up that suppliers often advise alternating one spray with another in an effort to prolong the effective killing power of the product.

Examining the case carefully, all that has really been achieved is the extermination of the pests' natural enemies, the introduction of a super-immune pest or, filling the vacuum created as a result of the destruction of the pest, a secondary pest may come to the fore and the cycle starts again.

The pests' natural enemies are dying out as modern civilisation exterminates them. If they do not die from being sprayed or poisoned by eating contaminated insects, then they are driven from their natural habitat by reclamation schemes and the removal of the hedgerows to make large agricultural expanses. The frogs, toads, birds and hedgehogs are all our friends in our fight to keep the crops pest free, yet we do not encourage them to live in the areas where their help is required most. The motor car also accounts for the loss of large numbers of hedgehogs each year.

How does all this affect us? The poisons are absorbed by the

13

plants and insects on which they fall, which are in turn eaten by the animals, birds and fish, which again in turn are eaten by us. Life is a chain, in which no one aspect can survive independently of the others. Just as the poisons are absorbed by the tissues of the plants, so the same is true of all living tissue, the insects, animals, birds, fish and man. Our bodies were not built to handle such materials so they are absorbed into our body fat or are collected by our kidneys and liver as they cleanse the body of toxins. These toxins build up, creating allergies and unexplained maladies. Some of the materials extensively used are carcinogenic.

The common practice of aerial spraying causes widespread distribution of the poison, as it can be carried by the wind over areas far greater than the user intended. For example D.D.T., the once 'miracle' product because of its persistent effects from small residual deposits, but later restricted in use due to the high levels being built up in the body, has now contaminated our earth to the extent that no part has eluded the product. Even the penguins in the Antarctic contain traces in their body fat – no one has been spraying there!

The effects are not restricted to one generation, but many, as the contaminators are passed on through the mother to affect another generation. When the newborn baby arrives it is already suffering from the effects of an intake of chemicals.

There are cases every year of people being poisoned by the wrong application, misuse or careless disposal of agricultural chemicals. Who can forget the disastrous consequences of the accidental release at Seveso, in Italy, of dioxin, used in the herbicide 245T, which is readily available from all garden supply centres?

There are methods of control available as well as non-toxic sprays which all lead to a safer and better edible product and environment. Left to her own ends, nature will offer a control over pests and in some respects we can accept this. There is plenty for all and provided the pests do not do irreparable damage then we can all live happily together.

Fertilisers

The aim of all gardeners is to replenish the soil with the food taken out by the plants in the previous season, in readiness for the coming year. The chemical gardener does this by adding artificial fertilisers, whereas the organic gardener does it by using only products produced by natural processes.

But why the difference? Let us look at the two fundamentals of growth, soil condition and plant nutrition.

Soil condition

We all know different soils look different. I feel it is fairly easy to decide which look in good condition and which do not, and in the process of deciding we hear terms such as 'soil structure' and 'tilth'. Soil in good condition balls when squeezed in the hand, yet breaks up easily when rubbed between the fingers. It is able to do this because it is made up of crumbs.

It is the ability of the soil particles to form these crumbs which is of the utmost importance in maintaining the soil in good condition, for it is these which help to build up a structure which will produce a good tilth. Crumbs are formed by the single-grain particles being held together by substances called 'colloids', and one of the most important of these is a material called 'humus'.

Let me deviate slightly at this point to clear up any misunderstanding of the definition of 'humus'. Humus and compost are not one and the same thing. Very simply, compost is what we call organic matter and is added to the soil. Organic matter may be in the form of vegetable compost, farmyard or stable manure, or leafmould, whereas humus is partially decomposed organic matter intermingled with the soil particles. The easy way to remember the difference is that you can physically add organic matter to the soil, but you cannot add humus. Humus is the middle product in the complicated chain of turning organic matter into plant food. Organic matter adds to the soil the essential elements for plant growth; humus is essential for its effect upon the soil structure and its ability to retain moisture.

The rate of decomposition of organic matter is increased in well-aerated soils, such as those being continually disturbed by cultivation, and as previously mentioned the compost is being broken down into humus which itself is being broken down into the essential plant foods, all of which is being carried out by the worms and bacteria present in the soil. So it is clear that if there is no replenishment then eventually all the humus is lost, resulting in the loss of its colloidal effect, the breakdown of the crumbs and the destruction of the soil structure back to single-grain particles. The effects of this soon become noticeable. The soil packs under heavy rain, moisture is not retained in dry periods and in extreme cases, soil erosion occurs.

Other important factors of humus are that it acts as a sponge, holding moisture and nutrients and darkening the soil which enables it to warm up more quickly in the spring and retain its heat. The importance of humus was summed up by the late Dr Sewell-Cooper when he said, 'Humus is to the soil as blood is to man.'

Now chemical fertilisers do not add organic matter. All they are is a plant food, and not a well-balanced one at that, as they provide only a limited number of the elements essential for healthy plant growth. Chemical fertilisers are mainly nitrogen, phosphorus and potassium, often referred to by their chemical symbols, N P K. They do not contain the trace elements so vital to the human body such as iron, boron and zinc.

Plant nutrition

Let us consider the nutritional aspects of organic as against chemical cultivation. For a plant to give you the full benefit of the nutritional value of a food, then the nutrients must be in the plant in the first place. To understand this it is necessary to have a look at how a plant feeds. It does so by two methods: through the leaves, taking in the gases – oxygen and carbon dioxide, and the elements presented by foliar feeds – and by the roots.

The roots take in the food in three ways. They are covered with unicellular hairs, commonly known as root hairs, whose function is to absorb water and the mineral salts in the soil. These mineral salts exist in the soil in an insoluble state and require to be converted into solution before they can be absorbed by the plant.

The life of the roots hairs is very limited, from a few days to weeks, and as they die they release protein and carbohydrates. Living in the soil are bacteria which take up the protein and carbohydrates and in the process of converting them into food also convert the insoluble minerals into solution which the plant can absorb. So both live happily together. These bacteria, however, require organic matter to exist so if there is no organic matter present then there is a reduced level of bacterial activity, and the process slows down or does not take place at all.

Chemical fertilisers do not add organic matter to the soil, and it is also known that they suppress the bacterial activity even more. Pesticides and herbicides are also known to kill off the bacteria.

The second method of food intake is by fungi living on the roots, exchanging food from root secretions for phosphates converted by the fungi from the soil. Again the fungal activity is suppressed or is killed off by applications of chemicals.

The third method of root feeding is by the transpiration current, that is the movement of water from the roots up to the leaves. This water contains the mineral materials which the plant stores and then removes when required. In the case of chemical feeding this is the *only* method by which the plant absorbs these chemicals and as they are very soluble then the plant can take in large quantities.

Problems of chemicals

As the chemical fertiliser is not a balanced feed, so another problem of using these fertilisers is the creation of an imbalance in the soil. When a large quantity of NPK is added in a form readily available to the plants, their demand for all the elements they require to maintain a balanced food intake increases. As long as all the requirements are available then healthy plants are obtained, but once one of the trace elements becomes in short supply then the plant growth is limited to the availability of that element. Thus we can see how the ground can become depleted of plant foods other than the three in the fertiliser.

Like humans, healthy plants will not grow on an unbalanced diet, so eventually we hear the chemical grower talk of mineral deficiencies. Impoverished soil can only supply impoverished food.

Chemical fertilisers also have two other factors against them. One is that incorrect application can do more harm than good. An overdose can be very damaging; any fertiliser falling on the foliage can result in scorching, even to the extent of the plants dying.

Secondly, studies in this field are showing the agricultural industry to be over-applying fertilisers to the tune of a million pounds a year. All this is paid for by the general public in food prices and the taxes which go towards growers' subsidies.

There is an even more serious consequence of the high level of chemical fertilisers used which has been highlighted by the work of the late Dr Geoffrey Taylor. He linked the excessive use of nitrogenous fertilisers, which produced crops containing high levels of nitrate and low levels of vitamin C, with stomach cancer.

It is very difficult to avoid the intake of these chemicals, for, once they have been applied to the land, their effects are far reaching. We either eat the crops directly, or they are fed to animals which eventually end up on the dinner table. Even our drinking water is contaminated as the rain leaches the fertilisers out of the soil into the streams. In extreme cases the surrounding environment can be destroyed, as was the case with Loch Leven which in 1967 eventually became devoid of anything living, due to the pollution from the surrounding fields.

So it can be seen that the continual use of chemical fertilisers will result in the eventual destruction of the soil structure, the growing of plants deficient in the essential vitamins and trace elements, and the absorption by our bodies of the chemicals applied which can be detrimental to our health.

Compost and the organic fertilisers, such as the seaweed products, are natural, well-balanced products without the disadvantages of the chemical equivalent and are therefore safe to use.

Chemical or organic – how to tell?

Just by reading the ingredients on the labels of the various products at the garden centre it is fairly easy to differentiate between the chemical and the organic. However, there are a number of products which strictly speaking are not organic, but are extensively used, and in these cases it is up to the individual which he accepts or rejects.

To help with the decision let us consider again how a plant feeds – the criteria for turning the nutrients into solution for absorption by the plant. I explained how the chemical fertiliser went easily into solution, so feeding the plant directly. The organic product, being less soluble, required the efforts of the soil bacteria and fungi to convert it into solution. In this case the process is to feed the soil, then the plant.

From this I can differentiate between a chemical and an organic product according to their solubility. Anything dissolving readily in water I would call a chemical; the not-so-soluble I consider safe to use. I will probably start no end of argument over that statement, but one must lay down ground rules and these are mine.

Chapter Two

Keeping the soil healthy

Our aim must be, by natural means, to replenish the food taken out by the plants and, if at all possible, more than compensate for the nutrients used so that the fertility of the soil can be built up to its highest level. We should endeavour to leave the soil in a better condition than we found it.

All this is achieved by the addition of organic matter to the soil and as with most aspects of horticulture there is more than one way of carrying this out. You can dig in the organic matter, but I feel there are several disadvantages to this method. Why bury the food 25 cm (10 in) beneath the soil when the plants require it in the top 10 cm (4 in)? Every time you disturb the soil, weed seeds are brought to the surface to become a nuisance later in the season. Digging can be hard work, too, so why add to your burden? I work the no-digging method and all my material is laid on the top of the soil in the form of a mulch. A spade plays a very small part in my garden.

Again, there are various ways of tackling the no-digging method. For instance, there is Ruth Stout with her 'no-work' system, involving the continual layering of spoilt hay on the soil coupled with all the garden waste, anything up to 60 cm (2 ft) thick. She does have the advantage of a readily available source of cheap hay to enable her to do so. My experience of her system did not meet with very much success, for in my part of the country hay is scarce and very expensive, so I compromised and used straw (which I still had to buy). Apart from an immediate explosion in the slug population, and the scattering of the straw around neighbouring gardens one stormy night, the major problem was the sudden death, for no apparent reason, of newly planted-out crops. The only cause I could think of was that there might still be sufficient weedkiller residue in the straw to affect the plants. However, having said that, do not let me put you off, for I have a colleague who can acquire hay and the system works very well for him. If you don't try out new ideas then you will never find what is best for you and your garden.

One of the most important lessons to learn in gardening is to find a system which suits the gardener and his soil. Every person and every garden is different and requires individual assessment. My system uses compost, which is the best starting point from which to build your own expertise.

Compost making

Now what can be converted into compost? Well, any material of vegetable origin can go into the system, and I feel it is very obvious which materials should be excluded – metals, man-made products such as plastic bags and fabrics, hard wood prunings and diseased material. Everything else, from your garden waste, kitchen waste, daily newspaper, hair and nail clippings, feathers out of old pillow cases, to the waste from your local greengrocer (shop waste) can all be broken down to feed your soil.

One of the items added to the compost is weeds out of the garden, and many people complain that their compost only spreads weeds. It is not the fault of the compost, but of the compost maker, in the failure to meet the requirements necessary to make good compost. So before rushing out to start a compost system, it is important to understand the processes involved in the conversion of your waste.

The main requirements for decomposition are air, heat and moisture. The initial stages are carried out by the aerobic bacteria and fungi, so it is essential to have plenty of oxygen (air) available. Lack of oxygen at this stage causes putrefaction of the decaying material, with the resultant unpleasant smell. Moisture is necessary in the lives of these aerobic bacteria and fungi, but an excess will prevent good aeration of the heap which again will encourage putrefaction. Heat is generated during the early days of decomposition, and temperatures as high as 82°C (180°F) can be reached. Heat encourages the bacteria to multiply and go about their good work.

Heat also plays another important role, that of sterilisation. To destroy weed seeds and diseased material, temperatures of 49 to 71°C (120 to 160°F) are required. Hence it is understandable why badly made heaps, which do not generate sufficient heat to sterilise the ingredients, are the carriers of weeds and even of disease. The later stages of the compost-making process are carried out by anaerobic bacteria (those not requiring oxygen) and the worms, and don't forget the activator, a source of nitrogen which assists the bacteria in the production of nitrates and which is the main form of food absorption by the plant.

The conventional method of making compost was to set aside an area of up to, say, 2.5 to 3 m (8 to 10 ft) long by 1.25 to 2 m (4 to 6 ft) wide and to start building up layers of waste, adding activator every 15 cm (6 in) and watering if the material was dry. This would be continued until the heap was 1.25 m (4 ft) high, when it was covered to keep the heat in and the rain out. This system is still in use and I have seen some first-class compost produced by it. But for the small garden it does have several disadvantages.

1. To maintain the heat and the moisture within the heap it should be built quickly, within one to two days. I have difficulty in collecting and storing sufficient material to enable this to be carried out.
2. As oxygen is an essential element, the heap needs turning after two to three weeks. This is a mammoth task which also requires space, and space is at a premium in a small garden.
3. It will be six to nine months before this compost is ready to use and there is always a percentage on the outside of the heap which has not rotted down and needs to be recycled.

What the owner of a small garden requires is to be able to compost small amounts of material as and when available, and to have converted them into a useable condition within three months.

Choosing a site
To maintain the conditions necessary to operate a good compost-making system care must be taken in the building and siting of the system.

The first consideration is the site. The ground should be as level as possible to ensure stability of the heap. The base must be soil, not concrete, as in the later stages the worms will be encouraged to play their part. Access is very important, for not only will you be bringing in the waste materials which initially may be in buckets or polythene bags, but at the end of the day your barrow will be required to cart away your compost. Don't forget to take into account where you will be spreading the compost – a compromise of all these three factors must be considered. It is no use having a convenient spot for bringing in materials if it is far away from the final spreading area. Then of course, as in my case, for the sake of my own household and also the neighbours, the cosmetic side is important. The area can be fenced off, and these fences make good supports for climbing plants. Unsightly smelly heaps do not usually result in good compost, nor in good relations with the neighbours.

The simplest and most effective way of making compost is to use a proprietary compost bin for the initial stages. Most will hold about .198 to .283 cu m (7 to 10 cu ft), which I find is about the amount I can collect each week. However, care must be taken in the choice of such a bin, for though some are good, others are not. We must not forget the three essentials for compost making – air, heat and moisture. Some of these bins have holes in the sides to allow air into the heap, but I believe these have a detrimental effect for all that they do is let the cold in and make it impossible to build up the heat. All the air necessary can be entrapped by turning over the contents at regular intervals. Make sure there is a good-fitting lid to keep out the rain and that the construction is such that the bin is stable and not easily knocked down or blown over by the wind. These bins, if well looked after, will last for several years.

I use the Rotol and Compostabin type bins to carry out the first stages of compost making. The bins are conical in shape and of lightweight construction, making it easy to lift them up and leave their contents intact on the soil. The difference between the two bins is the material of construction and their size. The Rotol holds .283 cu m (10 cu ft) of waste, whereas the Compostabin holds .198 cu m (7 cu ft). They are both the same price, so the choice is one of length of life versus capacity, the Compostabin having a slightly longer life span than the Rotol.

The first stage
The procedure is very simple. Place the bin on the soil in the composting area and have sufficient material available to fill it. I put some newspapers inside the bin first as I find this makes it

23

easier to collect all the rotted material when turning over the heap. Start layering in the waste with a generous dusting of calcified seaweed every 10 to 15 cm (4 to 6 in). Examine the waste being added, for if you use large amounts of vegetable waste a great deal of water will be released during the rotting-down process. If a quagmire around the bin is to be avoided, you will need to add some absorbent material to soak up this water. Grass cuttings or weeds are ideal, but if neither is available then newspapers or egg trays are just as effective. Layer the absorbent material every 10 to 15 cm (4 to 6 in), and continue until the bin is filled to the top.

Do not compress the material to push a bit more in, but put anything left over into a polythene sack till the next filling. Replace the lid and leave for seven to ten days. Do not add any more material after the initial filling.

As you will only fill the bins once a week, keep the waste material in polythene sacks (old fertiliser bags are ideal) until ready to use. Take the bags in rotation to ensure putrefaction does not start inside, causing unnecessary smells and inconvenience. With weeds, knock as much of the soil off the roots as possible before adding them to the bins, as soil is a cold material and it takes a lot of heat out of the bin to warm it up. The best way of handling weeds is to store them for two or three weeks in a polythene sack so that they start to rot down. The soil will then separate from the roots much more easily.

At the end of the seven- to ten-day period you will find the level in the bin has dropped to about one third to one half full. This will depend greatly upon the weather conditions, for during the very cold winter months the drop in level will be much less. The contents of the bin is starting to lose its appearance and there will be signs of a great deal of water being released.

At the end of seven to ten days lift off the bin and place it beside the heap. Put more newspaper in the bottom and then refill it with the now semi-rotted material, loosening it up as it goes back into the bin to entrap plenty of air. You will also be aware at this stage of the amount of heat being generated within the bin. After turning, replace the lid. No more calcified seaweed is needed. Do not add more fresh material, but leave it for another seven to ten days. When the bin is removed for a second time the heap will be even smaller and the contents almost unrecognisable.

The first stage of composting is now complete. A sufficiently high temperature has been reached within the bin to sterilise the contents and air has been entrapped to encourage the aerobic bacterial activity so that the bulk has been reduced. The next stage is for the anaerobic bacteria and the worms to carry out their functions. The heap now only requires to be kept warm and protected from the rain. This is easily done either by simply covering the heap where it lies with black polythene, or placing it in a specially prepared container such as the New Zealand bin, which I will describe later.

You will have worked out by now that it has taken two to three weeks to produce no more than a small amount of material, so I recommend a two-bin system operated as follows. Fill bin 1 as above. After the first week fill bin 2 from bin 1, leaving bin 1 for filling with fresh material. After this you will require space for three bins. After week 2 remove bin 2 and turn the contents of bin 1 into the empty bin followed by the contents of bin 2, so leaving an empty bin for fresh material. Repeat this process for three or four weeks until you end up with a bin full of processed material which can then be put in the New Zealand bin or covered with black polythene. You are now ready to start again.

If you only have room for one bin (remember you will need space for two to allow for turning over) then a compromise has to be reached, where the contents of the bin are covered with black polythene after only one week. They are then turned over and the contents of the bin are added on the second week and the process continued, with the bin kept empty for filling with fresh material. This is obviously not as good as the two-bin method, but under the circumstances it is acceptable. After all, our aim is to make good compost by any means available.

One point I should make clear is that it is almost impossible to make sufficient compost to meet your needs. The more land you have the more compost you need, requiring more of your time and enormous quantities of waste. In the smaller garden to dedicate sufficient land to meet your needs will greatly restrict your growth area, so a compromise is needed, making as much as you can and using it as efficiently as you can to obtain the best results.

Week 1

Bin 1. Fill with fresh waste

Bin 2. Empty

Week 2

Bin 1. Refill with fresh waste

Bin 2. Filled from bin 1

Week 3

Bin 1. Refill with fresh waste

Bin 2. Lifted off to new site and filled with contents of both bins

Week 4

Bin 1. Refill with fresh waste

Bin 2. Lifted to new site and filled with contents of both bins

Week 5

Bin 1. Refill with fresh waste

Bin 2. Contents covered with black polythene or put into New Zealand bin

Bin 2. Filled from bin 1

COMPOST MAKING

The second stage

I have mentioned the New Zealand compost bin for the second stage of compost making. I like the bin as it keeps the compost in a defined area, utilising space more efficiently and being aesthetically more acceptable than a heap. These tend to sprawl over the ground as you build them up, using valuable space in the small garden, and black polythene is not the most attractive product to look at. The bins, 1 m by 1 m by 1 m (3 ft by 3 ft by 3 ft) are not too large and are built in pairs to allow one to be filled while the other is emptied. I process something in the region of two to two and a half tons of compost through my two Rotol bins and a pair of New Zealand bins every year.

A description of the construction of the New Zealand bins is given in Dr Lawrence Hills's books or can be obtained from the Henry Doubleday Research Association (H.D.R.A.) in their leaflet *Give Up Smoking Bonfires*. They are very easy to build: I used old 15 cm (6 in) floorboards obtained from a scrap wood merchant, cheaper and more stable than buying new wood, and I have also added a top covering to keep the excess rain out.

Mulching

Having made all this beautiful compost how do we use it? If, like me, you adopt the no-dig method, most of the material will be used as a mulch. The procedure for mulching is very simple – feed the ground with an organic fertiliser, one of the seaweed products, and cover this with opened-out cardboard boxes, but not the waxed or heavily coloured types. A layer of newspaper about five sheets thick is a good substitute, but again avoid the coloured glossy paper. On top of this cardboard or paper, cover with an 8 to 10 cm (3 to 4 in) layer of the compost, then cover it all with black polythene. The fertiliser replenishes the nutrients removed by the previously growing plants, the cardboard or newspapers suppress the weeds, the compost builds up the humus content in the soil and maintains a high level of soil fertility, and the polythene acts as a back-up suppressant in the event of the weeds growing through the cardboard or newspapers as well as protecting the soil over the winter period, keeping it warm and preventing the nutrients being washed out by the rain. This allows planting out to take place in the spring when other unprotected parts of the garden are unfit to work through being too wet or cold.

This mulching procedure is best carried out when the soil is moist. The moisture is retained by the polythene over the winter period and with the darkness and warmth, favourable conditions are created for the worms and the soil bacteria to break down and reduce the cardboard, newspaper and compost and take them into the top layers of the soil, giving a beautiful weed-free tilth ready for the coming season. However, if the soil is too dry before the mulch is laid down these conditions are not achieved so that when the polythene is lifted in the spring the cardboard and newspaper will not have been broken down nor the compost pulled into the top soil by the worms.

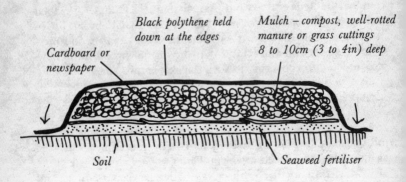

MULCHING THE SOIL

As the weeds will be suppressed by this method, there is no need to do any weeding before laying down the mulch – just cover and then forget about them. If by some chance they have grown tall, for instance where they have been hidden in the peas, then cut them down. Depending upon the weed and whether or not it is in a stage of seeding, it can be removed to the compost bins or just covered by the mulch.

Nature does not like bare soil and if left she will cover it with weeds, so I start my mulching programme in August when I begin to lift the summer crops, such as peas or cabbages, which are not being followed by a successional crop. As soon as an area large enough to cover becomes vacant, say from 2 m by 2 m (6 ft by 6 ft) upwards, then down goes the mulch, and as this area grows in size so the mulching continues. The polythene sheets come normally in 4 m (13 ft) widths, so if a length is cut sufficient to cover this width by the length of the plot, you can fold the polythene up in a convenient manner to cover the area being mulched and as the mulching extends then the polythene can be unfolded to cover the new area. In this way a great deal of time and effort is saved in the handling of the material. The polythene must be well held down to prevent it blowing away in the winter winds. This means you will need a supply of bricks, old fence posts, polythene bags filled with sand or anything to keep the sheeting in place until you are ready to lift it in the spring.

This mulching programme will continue through to December, by which time all mulching should be completed, as long as the ground is fit to work. Do not mulch in frosty weather because buried frost will remain frozen for some time, keeping the ground cold and delaying the start of planting out.

When lifting, do not remove all the polythene at once unless the ground is required immediately. The polythene can be folded back to expose the area needed for planting, while the rest of the plot remains protected. Do not remove any of the mulch when planting out; just dig a hole with the trowel or draw out a drill. The ground will be in perfect condition for growing.

Worm compost

This is an invaluable source of compost and can be made by anyone, no matter with what size of garden, even those who are only window-sill gardening. The objective is to provide a 'luxury hotel' for the manure worm (not to be confused with the earthworm), who in turn will convert your kitchen waste into a very rich compost. The principle and the building of the worm bin, using a standard domestic dustbin, is fully described in the booklet *Worm Compost* by Jack Temple, and is available from the Soil Association (see page 154).

This is not a compost-making process by bacterial activity but purely the waste digested by the worms. A worm eats approximately its own weight of food per day, and excretes a product very rich in the minerals nitrogen, potassium, phosphorus, calcium, and magnesium. As well as having a very high vegetable content, which is now in the form of a fine compost, the end product is so rich it needs to be diluted before coming into contact with the roots of plants.

There is no heat build up within the bin to sterilise diseased material or weed seeds, so care must be taken in what is added to the bin. The safest approach is to use only kitchen waste, no garden waste. However, it is surprising how many seeds are in kitchen waste, and many will germinate. In fact the first year I made worm compost I had a good collection of plants in the house all germinated in the worm bins – dates, lemons, apples, oranges and melons. Don't worry if the seedlings do grow, just pull them up – an easy task, for with growing in the dark they become very leggy, which gives them plenty of stem to get hold of. Put the seedlings in the Rotol bin. Even if pulled up and left on the top of the worm compost, the plant will continue to grow and be ignored by the worms as they will not eat anything living.

The worms require protein to breed and grow, and the easiest source of this is food scraps. It is perfectly safe to put these into the bin as it has a lid which will keep out animals and vermin. The best type of bin to use is the one which has handles to clip over the lid to hold it in place. I then tie the handles together as a secondary precaution. If food waste is not available then chicken mash is a good alternative.

Operating the system is very simple. Buy as large a dustbin as possible, remembering that the bottom 15 to 20 cm (6 to 8 in) are lost in establishing the correct living conditions for the worms. They need to be kept warm during the cold weather and if the bin is too small there is a chance of the contents freezing, as happened to one of my bins one winter.

Worms can be obtained from the fishing shop, sold as 'brandlings'. A margarine tubful is sufficient for starting one bin. Alternatively lay damp newspaper on the soil and a collection of little red worms will appear underneath. Pop these into the bin. Go gently at first and do not present the worms with too much food. A 15 cm (6 in) layer is enough until you see the worms on the top, then you can start building up the layers. Fork over the contents, mixing the new waste with the old. This helps to move the worms into the new waste which pushes the process along faster. I then cover the top surface of the bin with sedge peat to prevent a mould growing on the food scraps, and soak up excess moisture. Finish with a dusting of calcified seaweed.

Beware of using Irish peat for this brand can have a pH as low as 3 which will induce acid conditions in the bin and the enchytraeids will flourish instead of the worms. You will always have enchytraeids; they will gather in clumps around the acidic food in the bin, but generally their number will be small compared with the worms. If Irish peat must be used, then raise the pH by adding 225 g (8 oz) of calcified seaweed to a 9-litre (2-gal) bucketful of peat. You can dispense with the seaweed dressing in this case. Acid conditions can also be caused by too many banana skins and orange peel amongst the waste.

As the worms digest the food the level in the bin drops and at times you will begin to doubt if the bin will ever be full. I have found that the best system is to layer in the waste over a period until the bin is full. For an average family this may take three to four weeks. Cover with a 1 cm (½ in) thick layer of peat and turn this after a week. Do not add any more waste and if the contents look wet add some peat. Repeat this procedure for another three weeks, by which time the waste will be unrecognisable, but not yet fully digested by the worms: it will still be lumpy. At this stage it is semi-rotted, and there is a use for it in this condition which I will explain later.

Continue turning the bin once a week for a further four weeks. You will by this time have a dark, peat-like material. To keep the worms breeding, protein needs to be added during the turning periods, preferably in the form of breadcrumbs or a similarly textured material.

The bin is now ready to be emptied and another load started. Sieve the compost into a suitable container, say another dustbin, returning the coarse material retained in the sieve and as many worms as possible to the worm bin. Leave about a quarter of the bin contents as a starter for the next load, and repeat the cycle. You should be able to get three loads in a year as the process slows down over the winter months, taking from September to March to work out a bin.

The sieved material is now ready for use as a potting compost. Do not be surprised to see worms gathered round the lid and top of the container. It only means food has run out in the compost and they are looking for a fresh supply. Simply collect them and return them to the worm bin, where they can join their colleagues in digesting more waste.

The number of bins you have will depend upon your needs, available space and amount of waste from the household. I operate three bins and collect waste from neighbours, supplying them with a polythene bag which I collect when full. If the waste is not needed for the worm bins, remove the food and add the rest to the Rotol system. Always accept the quantity offered by a neighbour. To refuse appears to them to mean you no longer want the waste to be collected and the source dries up. The Rotol will handle all excess.

The fully worked worm compost is now ready to be used, but in its neat state it is too strong for seed sowing and transplanting of seedlings. I use it in the following proportions:-

Seed sowing mixture	1 part by volume worm compost 2 parts compost (out of New Zealand bin) 1 part sedge peat
Potting mixture	1 part by volume worm compost 1 part compost (out of New Zealand bin) 1 part sedge peat ½ part perlite Add 225 g (8 oz) calcified seaweed per 9-litre (2-gal) bucketful of the mixture

Use compost out of the New Zealand bin and put it through a 1 cm (½ in) sieve to remove the coarse material. Sedge peat can be replaced by Irish peat treated with 225 g (8 oz) calcified seaweed per 9-litre (2-gal) bucketful. Perlite is a water-absorbent material and will help to prevent the mixture drying out.

Comfrey

To the man in the street comfrey is no more than a weed, whereas in actual fact it is a wonder plant capable of providing food for man, animals and plants as well as playing an important role in herbal medicine. In some areas of the country it is referred to as 'knitbone', for it has remarkable properties for speeding up the mending of broken bones.

The roots of the plant can go down as far as 2 m (6 ft), gathering minerals and trace elements which are then stored in the stem and leaves. These are released when the comfrey is composted or converted into a liquid feed. The one drawback of growing comfrey in the garden, as with all deep-rooted plants, is that once it is there, it is very difficult to eradicate.

Dr Lawrence Hills has carried out an intensive study of the dozens of varieties of comfrey and concluded that the best for horticultural use is his classification Bocking 14 (the H.D.R.A. trial grounds are situated at Bocking, Essex, and each variety was numbered). Plants are available from the H.D.R.A. Dr Hills, in his book *Fertility Gardening*, goes into great detail about the analysis of comfrey, so all I will say here on the subject is that it is the richest known source of potash.

Comfrey can be used in the garden in many ways, the prime use being as a liquid feed, which can be made by two methods. The commonest is to add the stems and leaves to water, about 13.5 kg (30 lb) of leaf and stem to a 182-litre (40-gal) water barrel, and after three to four weeks this yields a feed ready for use. This method does have disadvantages; firstly, as the leaves are breaking down in the water some of the protein content is lost in the putrefaction, and secondly the resulting stench is appalling – not conducive to good relations with the neighbours. If the feed is made in a completely sealed container then the smell is greatly reduced, but it does tend to cling to hands and clothing when you use it. If the barrel is fed from the greenhouse or shed guttering, the concentration will be affected by rainfall, making it difficult to keep track of the strength and decide when to add more comfrey.

The better method is to make a comfrey press and squeeze the juice out of the leaves and stems. All you require is a container with a good-fitting lid, preferably of plastic, as metal ones rust. Any size will do from a bucket to a 182-litre (40-gal) water barrel. The larger it is the more juice can be extracted, but the more comfrey will be needed. Make a hole 1 to 2 cm (½ to ¾ in) in diameter either in the centre of the bottom or, as I prefer, in the side wall as near the bottom as possible. If you make the hole in the side wall, push a piece of plastic or copper tube through it to channel the juice into a collection pot. The tube must be a tight fit in the hole to stop leakage or prevent it from dropping out. The press can be placed on bricks to raise the bottom above the height of the collection container. A 4.5-litre (1-gal) fruit juice container is ideal for this purpose.

If the hole is in the bottom of the press, enlarge the hole in the collection pot by cutting away part of the top and place it directly beneath the hole in the press. If it is in the side wall, the outlet tube can be fed directly into the container mouth. Give both systems some form of protection from rain to prevent the juice from being diluted.

Fill the press with comfrey, placing on top a suitable heavy object such as a brick or piece of broken paving flag or stone, depending upon the size of the press. Replace the lid and in about two to three weeks a dark brown sweet-smelling liquid will start to drip out of the press. This is neat comfrey juice. Keep topping up with fresh comfrey to give a continuous supply of juice. I find filling a 91-litre (20-gal) container twice with comfrey produces 18 to 23 litres (4 to 5 gal) of the concentrated juice.

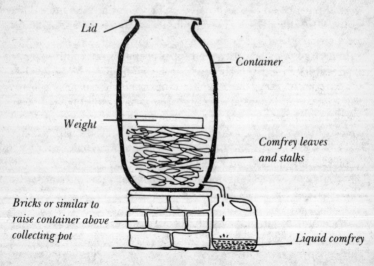

Lid

Container

Weight

Comfrey leaves and stalks

Bricks or similar to raise container above collecting pot

Liquid comfrey

LIQUID COMFREY MAKER

At the end of the season clean out the press, adding the remaining sludge to the compost, and the system is ready for the next year. The concentrated juice can be diluted between 10 and 40 times with water and used as a foliar feed on all plants and vegetables or as a liquid feed in the greenhouse and on house plants. I use a 30:1 ratio, as I prefer to feed weak but often. Mixing nettles with the comfrey in the press will enrich the juice even further.

Other than its use as a liquid, comfrey is excellent as a mulch. It is invaluable in the greenhouse on tomatoes when combined with worm compost. Potatoes also benefit from a comfrey mulch. Lay the leaves in the bottom of the trench before planting out the potato seed. Comfrey can also be added to the compost heap, but I feel this is a waste as its bulk reduces by about 10:1 and a load of comfrey produces very little compost.

The H.D.R.A. have a regular comfrey feature in their quarterly magazine reporting on the various uses of this remarkable plant and of members' experiments with it. One very good idea is making a soilless compost by layering peat and chopped-up comfrey. This needs to be made in a contained area. On a small scale I use a dustbin, or on a large scale a New Zealand bin. Fill the container with alternate layers of the peat and comfrey – about 10 cm (4 in) layers of each – and then leave it until the comfrey rots down. I find this an ideal product for mixing with worm compost for a seed sowing and potting compost.

Where comfrey is to be covered it is normally advisable to allow it to wilt for 24 hours before use, because there can be a tendency for the comfrey to take root. When circumstances have not allowed me to take this wilting time I have used comfrey freshly cut, keeping a look out for any signs of unwanted fresh growth, without any trouble at all.

Leafmould

Leaves must be treated separately from the other waste in the garden. They should not be added to the compost for they take a good while longer to rot down. In some cases this can be as long as two to three years. Not only that, but they do not generate heat during decomposition so any weed seeds present could survive to germinate again. If the leaves are mixed with ordinary compost they produce 'cold' areas within the heap and therefore restrict the amount of heat generated. Do not burn leaves: not only is this extremely wasteful of a very valuable product – the trees in our forests have lived solely on their own decaying leaves for generations – but also a nuisance to neighbours with the dense smoke such a fire makes and a smell which lingers on well after the fire is out.

There are two ways of dealing with leaves. The first is to make a leafmould cage by driving four stakes into the ground to make a square, then surrounding them with wire netting to form a cage. The dimensions will depend on the quantity of leaves available, but an average size is about 1 m (3 ft) cubed. Although many gardeners use only the wire netting, I put polythene sheeting on the inside of the netting to keep out the rain and cold. Place the leaves in the cage, watering them if dry, and about every 15 cm (6 in) tread down the layers. The rotting of leaves does not need air (oxygen) so pack them down hard, filling the cage to the top. Cover and leave. Leaves can be collected from a number of areas – the streets, parks, other people's gardens, but ask permission first. Some may contain twigs, paper, or polythene bags, so remove as much debris as possible when stacking. Just as you do not add leaves to garden compost you do not add garden waste to leaves. In about two years the stack will have reduced to about half its size by volume. After 12 months the stack is sufficiently consolidated to allow the posts and wire netting to be removed for the next collection of leaves.

The second method is to put the leaves in polythene sacks and add about one forkful of worm compost complete with worms – the more worms the better. Again it will take about two years to rot down.

The rotted leaves, or leafmould as it is commonly called, is not a manure for it contains little plant food. The nutrients are transferred back into the stems in the autumn. However, leafmould adds bulk to the soil, and eventually humus. As it is long lasting, whatever nutrients are left in the leaves are released slowly over a period of time, consequently this is ideal for sandy soils. Again I prefer to apply it as a mulch in the autumn rather than digging it in.

I also use the leafmould in potting composts, chopping it up with a spade and passing it through a 1 cm (½ in) sieve. The coarse pieces can either be used in a mulch or returned to the leaf cage to rot for another year.

Green manure

Nature retains the soil fertility by covering the ground with grasses and weeds, which at the end of their growing cycle rot down and return their goodness to the soil. This is the principle of green manuring, the growing of a crop with the sole purpose of returning it to the soil.

I do not recommend green manuring as an alternative to compost mulching, but it is ideal for the areas which are to be left vacant without mulching over the winter period. It has the advantage of preventing the nutrients being washed out of these areas by the rain, and gives a form of weed control as well as a source of organic material for adding to the soil.

Green manure crops are available for both summer and winter sowing, but in the small garden the summer-sown crops are not used for obvious reasons.

Seeds are sown in autumn, August to early October, and are left till March/April, by which time anything up to 45 cm (18 in) of growth will be available. The foliage can then be dug in or mown down and left to rot on the surface or may be removed and added to the compost heap.

Winter tares and Hungarian rye are the two most popular crops for autumn sowing. Alfalfa can be used if sown in the late summer, and mustard, which is really a summer crop, will survive the winter in certain areas. A word of warning about mustard, however: it is a member of the brassica family and is not recommended if club root is about or the plot has just grown or is about to grow the members of the cabbage group. Take good note of your crop rotation.

Seeds are available and can be obtained from the H.D.R.A. or Chase Seeds (see page 154 and 155).

Farmyard Products

Making compost involves a regular commitment to collect waste material and a certain amount of physical effort in turning the material at the Rotol stages and transferring it to the New Zealand bins. Not everyone is in a position to lift heavy loads and yet adding organic matter is of the utmost importance. Grass-cutting mulches go a long way to help, but the supply of this is limited to the growing season, whereas we still need compost throughout the year.

An alternative supply of material is from the farmyard in the form of cow, horse and poultry manures as well as straw. The manures can be purchased in bulk and barrowed into the garden and many farmers now sell it by the bagful. Straw does come in bales which are heavy to lift, but once delivered the baling string can be cut and the straw removed in small amounts.

The quality of the farmyard manures varies greatly according to the animals' diet and the type of litter used for their bedding. With the growing number of riding schools around the country the most widely available is horse manure, but unfortunately, the modern trend is away from straw towards sawdust and wood shavings for bedding. I do not recommend the use of manures containing either for they take many years and require a considerable amount of nitrogen to rot down, and this is usually robbed from the soil.

As with all materials to be composted the manures are best used when well rotted. It is inadvisable to use them in the fresh state. Always stack manure separately from the other compost heap and do not put it through the Rotol system. One of the New Zealand bins can be used or simply build a heap and cover it with black polythene. In either case build it up in 15 cm (6 in) layers, dusting liberally with calcified seaweed between each layer. If the manure is very dry water each layer when building up.

Poultry manure is very much 'hotter' than cow or horse manure and *must* be well rotted before use or considerable damage can be done to the roots of the plants.

Straw

With the modern battery farming methods the sources of cow and poultry manure are diminishing, and with the increase in the use of by-products from the wood industry for horse bedding the alternative is to use straw.

I prefer to compost the straw, which gives time for the chemicals to break down and the end product is less likely to blow in the wind. Do not dig in fresh straw. It does not contain any nitrogen and as this element is needed in the decomposition cycles, the nitrogen will be robbed from the soil and deficiency symptoms will result.

Divide the bales up into 15 cm (6 in) thick slabs, easily done by pulling the straw apart, and lay out flat in a 1.25 m (4 ft) square. The straw needs to be thoroughly wetted, and a nitrogen fertiliser such as dried blood or seaweed meal must be added to activate and promote decomposition. Poultry manure is very good if you can get it for it contains bacteria which specialise in breaking down the cellulose in the straw. Also add ground limestone or dolomite at a rate of 225 g per sq m (8 oz per sq yd) to neutralise the acids formed during the decomposition process. Then add a second 15 cm (6 in) layer of straw and repeat the process until the heap is about 1.25 m (4 ft) high.

Oxygen plays an important role in the early stages of decomposition. Sufficient air will be trapped in the straw, but do not tread down during the building of the heap – it will settle down under its own weight. Build the heap quickly, inside a day if possible, but not more than two, to prevent loss of moisture from the straw and to encourage the build up of heat for the initial stages of decomposition. When completed, cover it with black polythene sheeting held down firmly at the edges. Keep the polythene covering tight as the heap shrinks. If there is any sign of drying out soak the heap again thoroughly. There is no need to turn it over; just leave it and in about three months the centre will be ready to use as a mulch. Recycle the undecomposed outside portions in the next straw heap.

The end product is not as good as compost and I would not recommend it as a replacement if you can make compost.

Chapter Three

Organic fertilisers and the acid/alkali balance

The previous chapter placed great emphasis on soil fertility and the recycling of waste into compost for returning to the soil. The compost together with the seaweed fertilisers will supply the average needs for growth. But there are occasions when there are demands for individual elements, for instance to stimulate root growth, and as these needs cannot be met simply with compost and seaweed it is in circumstances such as these that we turn to the organic fertilisers.

The analysis of the pure organic fertilisers such as the seaweed products cannot be controlled or guaranteed for there are many factors involved in nature's manufacturing process. Any analysis quoted by a supplier therefore tends to be an average figure for their product. Even with the individual mineral fertiliser, such as bonemeal, despite more scope for control as it goes through a manufacturing process, it is common to find slight variations for the same named product sold by different manufacturers.

To the non-technical person, the analysis on the bag can be confusing, for not only are the elements referred to by their chemical symbol, but some are quoted in the oxide form. A full understanding of the jargon is not important; the main thing is to know which fertiliser is the best source of the particular element required. When comparing one fertiliser with another make sure the same form is being compared.

The following table will be useful:

Element	Chemical Symbol	As denoted in analysis
Nitrogen	N	N
Phosphorus	P	P_2O_5
Potassium	K	K_2O
Calcium	C	CaO
Magnesium	Mg	MgO

As well as these five elements the plant also requires a number of others to produce healthy growth. Many of these are only required in minute amounts and are referred to as 'trace elements'. They are all, however, vital components in the plant's life and are an essential inclusion in our diet if we are to maintain a healthy body. Their role in life is not the subject for a gardening book but for further reading on this subject I would recommend *You Are How You Eat* by Donald Law, published by Turnstone Books.

Let us now look at the various sources of these elements which are available to the organic gardener. One of the most important is seaweed. Its value lies in its richness in the trace elements, including many which are difficult to obtain from other sources. Being of living origin it is well balanced and safe to use, and the best material to ensure the soil does not suffer from nutrient deficiencies. Seaweed is available in a number of forms.

Fresh seaweed

Seaweed in its fresh state taken from the beach is not really a fertiliser but more a manure. It can be applied as a mulch and as the seaweed is richer in the early part of the year, is best used in the spring and early summer. If spread on the soil and left it does have a tendency to dry out and go brittle, but a covering of grass cuttings, compost or straw will help to preserve the moisture and prevent the smells which attract flies. Salt can be a problem, so the seaweed should be hosed down before being spread on the soil. If the seaweed is used in the autumn there is no need to wash out the salt as it will have been neutralised by the spring.

Fresh seaweed is best used by adding it to the compost heap. Let the seaweed dry out for 48 hours to lose a large proportion of its water content, otherwise the heap will become very wet, and putrefaction will take place with the resulting unpleasant smells. Layer it in the New Zealand bins with the general compost from the Rotol bins in 15 cm (6 in) layers of each. I like to put newspapers, egg trays or a 2.5 cm (1 in) layer of grass cuttings either side of the seaweed to absorb the water still to be lost during decomposition. Mix the bin contents thoroughly to ensure a good distribution of seaweed in the compost. Being very high in potash the seaweed compost is ideal for use in the greenhouse on the tomatoes.

It does have one disadvantage, however – transportation. Being very bulky it is difficult to carry, yet it rots down to nothing. It is usually wet, so use a polythene bag and tie the neck to prevent flooding the car. It has the advantage of being free of weeds, pests and diseases, but do watch out for oil contamination when collecting it.

Seaweed products

To meet the needs of the average gardener seaweed is obtainable in the more conventional forms of powder and liquid, and is readily available from the garden centre.

Each manufacturer uses a different variety of seaweed in their product, hence each has much to offer and quite often one will supplement the other when used in a combined application. One point all manufacturers agree upon is the beneficial effect seaweed has upon the soil and subsequently the plants. The seaweed encourages bacterial activity within the soil, the release of locked-up minerals and the development of good root systems, as well as supplying its own range of nutrients to build a high level of soil fertility.

One very important aspect of seaweed is its ability to improve poor or neglected soils, not only breaking down heavy clay, but on light, sandy soils helping to create a good crumb structure and better moisture retention properties.

The versatility of the seaweed products makes them indispensable in the garden.

Calcified seaweed (Seagold)

Unlike the other seaweed products which use living plants, calcified seaweed is the remains of dead seaweed and is lifted from the sea bed off the Brittany and Cornish coasts. The seaweed, which in its living form looks like coral, floats across the Atlantic in the Gulf Stream to be deposited as it dies in large quantities off these coasts. This seaweed has a great affinity for calcium, so that when dried and ground up it gives a product which has a very high calcium content as well as all the nutritional properties of seaweed. A high magnesium content enhances its value further. The result is a general fertiliser combining pH control with valuable nutrients.

As its acid neutralising effect is limited to pH 6, calcified seaweed is safe to use on such crops as potatoes which dislike alkaline conditions. To ensure my composts are of the correct pH level I add 225 g (8 oz) per 9-litre (2-gal) bucketful of compost. In this way I have made any acidity corrections needed as well as adding a general fertiliser.

Calcified seaweed is very much cheaper than the other seaweed solid products, so as a result I restrict the use of the more expensive ones to specific requirements, using the calcified seaweed as a general purpose fertiliser supplemented by organic fertilisers to compensate for its low phosphate and potash content.

Seaweed meal

Seaweed meal is produced from a bladder seaweed harvested from the beds off the northern hemisphere coastline. It is gathered by methods which leave the growing parts of the plants undamaged, so retaining their ability to continue producing growth to allow further harvesting. In this way the source is not depleted. The seaweed is dried and ground to produce the fine powdered meal.

Seaweed meal is of a very high nutritional value, not only for plants but also for animals, since it contains the major elements and trace elements as well as protein, carbohydrate, fat, the amino acids and many vitamins. The competition for its use unfortunately keeps the price high, being approximately twice the price of calcified seaweed. I use Maxicrop Seaweed Meal Horse Feed Supplement.

The advantage over calcified seaweed is that it contains nitrogen and is much higher in potassium, but loses out on the calcium, magnesium and phosphate levels. I use it as a general fertiliser in the autumn mulching programme. Before spreading the cardboard or newspaper on the soil I apply seaweed meal at a rate of 225 g (8 oz) per square metre (yard) supplemented with Alginure, and for the brassica plot dolomite or ground limestone. It would appear to be slower acting than the calcified seaweed and my experience has shown better results are obtained from an autumn application than from a spring application.

Maxicrop also produce a liquid seaweed for use as a foliar feed during the periods of high nutrient requirement in the growing season. Foliar feeds are assimilated faster by the plants as they do not have to go through the root feeding cycle. This gives a rapid boost to the plant at the times when its demands for certain nutrients are high.

Alginure

This is sold as a soil improver and is best used in conjunction with one of the other seaweed products applied at a rate of 14 g (½ oz) per square metre (yard). At this small rate mix it with the other product to give it bulk so that it will be easier to spread uniformly.

It is made from the brown wrack type of seaweed which is dried, milled, then processed into a material which has similar characteristics to humus, hence its ability to stimulate the soil bacterial activity, create soil crumbs and retain moisture.

I use all the seaweed products in conjunction with each other to ensure that the soil is maintained in a well-balanced, healthy condition. The seaweed products are good general fertilisers combining the four major plant foods with the essential trace elements. There are also fertilisers which contain only one or two of the major elements which can be used to compensate for a plant's greed for a particular element or to correct a deficiency.

Essential elements

My theme on feeding throughout this book is to maintain a balance and it may be felt that to use these single element fertilisers goes against this principle. Their use is restricted to meet the specific needs of certain plants, not for general application, and as these organic products are slow acting, releasing the element over a period, then the dangers which one would get with the concentrated chemical fertilisers do not exist.

A brief look at the role played by each element in the growth pattern will assist in the selection of the correct fertiliser.

Nitrogen (N) This is the basic element of life, essential for the main growth process of plants. As a major constituent of chlorophyll it is of particular value to the leaf producers, giving them their rich green colour. A shortage is shown by stunted growth and the production of unhealthy-looking leaves pale green to yellow in colour.

Potassium, or potash (K) Helps the growth process and is particularly important for the development of fruit, being useful to such crops as tomatoes. It is also an aid to building up a plant's resistance to disease.

A shortage can be the result of excessive use of nitrogen and phosphate fertilisers, showing up as the thinning of stems, leaves losing their colour and eventually withering, fruit lacking in colour and flowers with leaves showing signs of scorching round the edges. Potatoes turn black when cooked.

Phosphorus (P) Develops the root system, aids the ripening of seeds and fruit and the maturing of the plant. Shortage is shown by poorly developed roots and discoloured leaves. Sometimes it can be mistaken for a nitrogen deficiency.

Calcium (Ca) This element assists the growing functions of the plant, promotes root growth and neutralises the soil's organic acids. Symptoms of calcium deficiency are stunted growth; the growing tips of shoots become ragged, roots fail to develop and the plant becomes susceptible to disease. Blossom end rot on tomatoes can be the result of lack of calcium.

Magnesium (Mg) Works closely with phosphorus in the ripening of seeds and is essential for the formation of chlorophyll. Shortages are shown by stunted growth and the loss of colour in the leaves, the signs showing first on the older leaves, then moving slowly to the young leaves.

Trace elements Some of the more important trace elements are boron, copper, iron, manganese, molybdenum and zinc.

The fertilisers

Bonemeal This has been a very popular product with gardeners for many years and is the richest source of phosphorus with between 20 to 30 per cent phosphate. It is very slow acting, and best applied in the autumn at a rate of 225 g (8 oz) per square metre (yard). When made from raw bones it contains a little nitrogen, amounting to between 2 and 4 per cent.

Dried blood A very fast-acting fertiliser with a high nitrogen content of 12 per cent. Rate of application is 25 g (1 oz) per square metre (yard), and because of its quick release of nitrogen it is best used in early spring to mid summer.

Blood, fish and bonemeal This is a combination fertiliser containing 2 to 5 per cent nitrogen, 5 to 8 per cent phosphate and 0.5 to 6 per cent potassium. Applied at a rate of 110 g (4 oz) per square metre (yard) in the spring, the quick release of nitrogen from the blood encourages plant growth, while the phosphate being released slowly over a period develops a strong root system.

Hoof and horn meal Another high nitrogen fertiliser averaging a 13 per cent nitrogen content, but much slower acting than the dried blood. It makes a valuable addition to the potting compost. When transplanting lettuces and cabbages into paper pots add 25 g (1 oz) to the 9-litre (2-gal) bucketful of compost, or as a general feed apply at 110 g (4 oz) per square metre (yard).

Rock potash The source for a long-lasting effect, containing 10 per cent potash. It can be applied at any time of the year at 225 g (8 oz) per square metre (yard), one application lasting two to three years.

Rock phosphate Contains 13 per cent phosphate which is released over a number of years. A single dressing lasts a long time. Apply at a rate of 225 g (8 oz) per square metre (yard).

As a general guide 1 handful of fertiliser equals 55 g (2 oz).

All the fertilisers are expensive, some of those containing the individual elements even more so than the seaweed products. Great savings can be made by buying the largest bag available, usually a 25-kg (56-lb) bag, which will cut the cost by as much as half. If this size is too large, share a bag with your gardening colleagues. Heavy postage rates makes mail order very unattractive. Garden centres sometimes stock the large bags or will order them for you, but failing that the commercial wholesaler will sell you a bag provided you collect and buy the stock size. Fertilisers will keep for a number of years if stored correctly.

If your requirements do not merit purchasing these individual fertilisers then the alternative is to go for a general purpose one such as PBI's 'Back to Nature' with an analysis of 7.3 per cent nitrogen, 5 per cent phosphate and 5.2 per cent potash. It is ideal for the person with a very small garden and limited facilities. Incidentally, the 'Back to Nature' range also includes organically made insecticides.

For the very small garden where compost making is out of the question, the alternative is to use the organic proprietary compost and manures such as those supplied by Clavering Organics Real Gardening Ltd (see page 155). Their mushroom compost and peat manure offer all-round products for mulching the small garden. As well as supplying the individual mineral fertilisers a complete fertiliser is available containing 3.5 per cent nitrogen, 8 per cent phosphate and 10.5 per cent potash.

Two products which must be mentioned are dolomite, with 30 per cent calcium and 22 per cent magnesium, also called magnesium limestone, and ground limestone with 55 per cent calcium. Both are used for soil pH correction, the organic gardener's answer to lime. The work I have carried out shows both will raise the pH value to 6.5, dolomite being the superior product for its magnesium content. An application of 225 g (8 oz) per square metre (yard) will last for about two years.

One other product which appears in the potting compost is perlite. This is expanded volcanic rock. It is not a plant food but an aid to growth, being a good substitute for the sharp sand and grit used in conventional compost mixes. It is valuable for opening up the structure of the compost and so improving the aeration and drainage. Being sterile, it is also weed and disease free. The added advantage is its water-holding properties, as it absorbs water then releases it when required, preventing the compost from drying out too quickly. As it is inert it does not deteriorate, but retains its properties throughout the life of the compost.

The acid/alkali relationship

The principles and chemistry of soil management are very complex and not the subject for this book. However, one aspect is of the utmost importance, that being the acid/alkali relationship, often referred to as 'sourness' or more commonly the pH of the soil.

Though strictly speaking the pH is a measure of the level of hydrogen-ion concentration in solution, for practical purposes it is used as an indication of the acidity/alkalinity balance in the soil on a scale running from pH 0 to pH 14. In horticulture, plant growth will only occur between pH 3.5 and pH 8, pH 6.5 to pH 7 being the optimum range for vegetable growing (see page 52).

It is a fact of life that the soil over most of Britain is naturally acidic. A typical slice through uncultivated soil would show that over a spade's depth the average is approximately pH 4, and the majority of the materials we will distribute on the soil throughout the growing period, the animal manures and compost, are all acid biased and will maintain the soil in an acidic condition.

Even pure natural rain is acidic, having a value of pH 5.6, but if you live in an industrial area, the rain will be polluted by chimney effluent and drop as low as pH 4.

All this means that steps must be taken to correct the imbalance and return the soil to the horticultural neutral of pH 6.5.

The pH level is important for the soil is extremely sensitive to any changes in acidity which will modify its physical and chemical condition and so change the distribution and activity of the soil bacteria, which in turn affect the nutrition of the plants.

Every plant has a pH range outside which it will not grow, but within this range there is a much narrower band corresponding to optimum growth. The majority of vegetables have an optimum range mean of pH 6.5. Hence, this is the value for the 'horticultural neutral'.

The solubility and availability of mineral nutrients is greatly influenced by changes in pH, for as alkalinity increases over pH 6.5 then such nutrients as nitrogen, phosphorus and potassium become less available while iron becomes totally unavailable. As the alkalinity drops below the pH 6.5 unit value and the soil becomes more acid, then again nitrogen, phosphorus and potassium become less available, calcium becomes totally unavailable, but iron, aluminium and manganese became available in excess to the extent that toxicity symptoms can occur.

It can be seen how relatively small changes in the soil pH can affect the growth of the plants, and as the requirement of each plant differs then a change of 1 to 2 in the unit of pH can retard the growth of certain plants, while encouraging the growth of others. Look how heathers and bracken flourish on acid soils while little else will grow there.

The availability of soil nutrients is closely linked with the level of activity of the soil bacteria, which themselves are sensitive to changes in acid/alkali levels. Although, like plants, capable of existing over a wide range, they too have an optimum range of pH for maximum activity.

The most important bacteria are those associated with the 'nitrogen cycle'. This is the continuous process of converting organic material into plant food and depends upon a succession of bacteria each carrying out a stage in the transforming of organic nitrogen into ammonia and then to nitrates for absorption by the plants. At pH 6 and above the bacteria associated with nitrification and ammonification work at about the same level of activity; below this value the level of nitrification activity decreases until it eventually ceases at about pH 4.5. Hence the reason for the smell of ammonia from badly made compost heaps and fresh animal manures – they are too acid.

Perhaps the most sensitive bacteria are those fixing free nitrogen from the atmosphere (Azobacter). Their activity is restricted to a very small range with optimum activity at pH 7.0 to 7.2, dropping off rapidly till activity completely ceases at pH 6.

The pH level is also closely associated with the incidence and severity of plant diseases, the best known example being club root, the savage of the brassica family. This disease is very persistent in acid soil, but is very rare in alkaline soils.

On the other hand potato wart and scab diseases are more prevalent on alkaline soils and considering optimum growth occurs at below pH 6, there is good sense in the old saying to keep lime and potatoes as far apart as possible.

There are links between all aspects of acid/alkaline influence, as many instances of disease can be related to plant nutrition and to plant growth, which can in turn be related to soil pH.

Soil testing

There are a number of ways of checking your soil acidity. First of all there is the schooldays' method of using litmus papers, although times have changed since my childhood and the red and blue papers have been replaced by one covering the full range of pH 0 to pH 14. These are very simple to use and accurate enough for our purposes.

This method requires a soil solution to be made up and for comparison purposes it is important always to treat each sample in an identical way. Using the same measure, take about 25 g (1 oz) of soil, add 20 cc (1 fl oz) of water and stir for five minutes. By doing this, one sample can be directly compared with any other.

Then there are the pH meters giving a direct reading. These are very much easier to use than the pH paper but have the disadvantage of being relatively expensive.

Alternatively, there are the proprietary kits available from the garden centres, coming in two sizes, either determining pH only or with means of indicating nitrogen, phosphorus and potassium levels as well. Again, these are very simple to use with easy-to-follow instructions, including a list of pH ranges for common plants and vegetables.

If the soil does require correction this is achieved by dosing it with calcium. This is where you will probably meet the problem of deciding what is a chemical and what is not, for the common product for neutralising soil is lime, and this is accepted by recognised organic gardening bodies as suitable for use. Lime, or hydrated lime as it is sometimes labelled, is made by adding water to quicklime, itself produced by heating limestone to very high temperatures. The question is – does this constitute a chemical process? I accept wood ash as a suitable material and that is a product of combustion, so why not lime? After all, it will be used as a soil conditioner, not a plant food. The answer lies in the definition given in Chapter 1. Lime is very soluble, so I regard it as a chemical product.

To substantiate this decision, work I carried out to determine the rates of application of calcium-containing products for pH correction showed the dangers of using soluble materials. (See facing page). Taking a 9-litre (2-gal) bucketful of Irish moss peat of pH 3 as a standard, the addition of 55 g (2 oz) of hydrated lime increased the pH to 8, 110 g (4 oz) gave pH 9.5 and 170 g (6 oz) gave pH 11. An average handful is 55 g (2 oz). Accidental over-application is now doing a great deal of damage.

However, the organic products, calcified seaweed, magnesium, limestone (dolomite) and ground limestone, were shown to be very safe to use. The pH of the peat increased steadily until 285 g (10 oz) per 9-litre (2-gal) bucketful gave pH 6 to 6.5. Any further increase in the calcium product gave no further increase in pH. Accidental over-application does no more than waste your money.

Converting these figures to ground applications, I recommend a rate of 225 g (8 oz) per square metre (yard) for all three products.

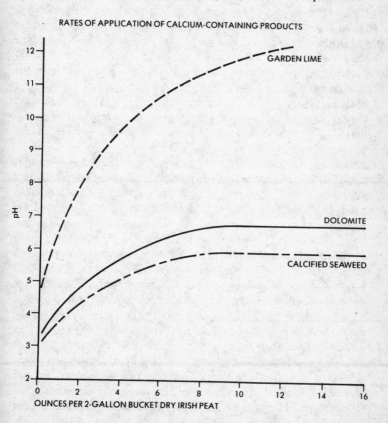

RATES OF APPLICATION OF CALCIUM-CONTAINING PRODUCTS

Optimum pH range for vegetables

Artichoke, Jerusalem	6.5–7.5
Beans – broad, French, runner	6.0–7.0
Beetroot	6.0–7.5
Broccoli	6.5–7.5
Brussels sprouts	6.5–7.5
Cabbage	6.5–7.5
Calabrese	6.5–7.5
Capsicum (sweet pepper)	5.5–7.0
Carrots	5.5–7.0
Cauliflower	6.5–7.5
Celery	6.0–7.0
Courgette	6.0–7.0
Cucumber	5.5–7.5
Kale	6.5–7.5
Leeks	6.0–7.0
Lettuce	6.0–7.0
Marrow	6.0–7.0
Onion	6.0–7.0
Parsnips	5.5–7.0
Peas	6.0–7.5
Potato	4.5–6.0
Spinach	6.0–7.5
Swede	6.5–7.0
Tomato	5.5–7.0
Turnip	6.0–7.0

Chapter Four

Planning the vegetable garden

Having looked at plant nutrition and soil maintenance, the next point to consider is what is to be grown? Before buying seeds there are several questions which need to be asked.

1. Which vegetables do you want to grow and over what period of the year? Are you going to grow during the summer months only or consider a 12-month supply out of the garden?

2. Are the vegetables chosen compatible with the area? For example, sweet corn is not a suitable crop for a garden in the North whereas beetroot, for instance, is ideal. The object is to provide the basis of a chemical-free diet, not a bowlful of exotic products.

3. What varieties grow best in the area? For the beginner valuable assistance can be obtained from more experienced gardeners as to suitable varieties for the climatic conditions.

4. Is the soil suitable for the selection? It may require a compromise for the first few years until poor or neglected soil has been raised to a good level of fertility – cauliflower, for instance, requires a very rich organic soil. Planting it in poor soil will give no return and waste time, effort and growing space.

5. What weather conditions are likely throughout the season? Early crops may require protection with cloches, and if the area is subject to high winds then tall varieties have either to be well staked or avoided.

Having answered the above questions a work programme must be considered for each of the seasons, for the few moments spent planning ahead can more than pay for themselves during the busy growing periods.

Winter (November, December, January, February)

This is the time for reflecting upon the previous season's perform-ance, noting the successes and the crops which were not so

CROPPING PLAN

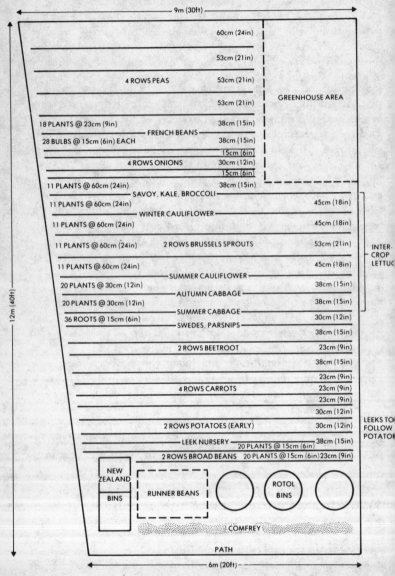

successful, and asking yourself what went wrong. What can be learnt from the mistake and what is required next year?

A plan of the garden should be laid out showing where each plant family will go, putting down distances between rows to ensure you can fit everything into the available space and showing the distances between plants to enable you to calculate the number of plants you can grow and still allow intercropping and successional sowing to take place. Do not forget about crop rotation, a very important consideration particularly in a small garden.

The seed catalogues drop through the letter-box during the weeks leading up to Christmas, and I spend many an enjoyable hour engrossed in their pages, reminiscing on the tasty products enjoyed and still being enjoyed out of the garden, and in the selection of the vegetable seeds for the coming season, and looking forward to yet another bumper harvest.

I like to introduce one or two new varieties each year to grow alongside the old faithfuls, not only to ensure I am growing the best but so that each year, as I find yet another of the old ones has disappeared from the catalogue, I am in a position to grow a proven substitute. Also many of the new varieties do have a great deal to offer, particularly with respect to disease resistance. Do not be afraid to try new varieties and growing techniques. I cannot emphasise this point too strongly, but remember, if things do not work out as planned, there is a lesson to be learnt and this must be borne in mind for future years.

I recommend growing everything from seed. A number of gardeners argue against this for the small garden, where only a limited number of plants of each variety will be planted, reasoning that plants from the garden centre are more economic and convenient. My reply is that seeds, if stored correctly, will keep for a number of years, so the initial purchase price is spread over these years. Also, if you are considering successional sowing, a regular supply of plants is required over a period of time. The garden centre only supplies plants as and when available and not always when you require them. Very often the variety of a bought plant is unknown, a very important point if we are looking for a supply over an extended period, for there are few rewards from planting an early variety for a late crop and vice versa.

Another crucial factor against bought plants is the importing of disease. I speak from experience, when several years ago I bought cabbage plants which turned out to be infected with club root. It is important, however, to make sure you buy good-quality seeds from a reputable seedsman.

Winter is also maintenance time, when any necessary repairs should be carried out on the greenhouse, cold frames and fencing. Pots and trays will need to be thoroughly washed and stacked in a safe place, preferably under cover of the greenhouse or shed to prevent them being blown around by the wind or becoming the wintering grounds for pests. Tidy up canes and stakes, wash if necessary and again store in a safe manner. Bits and pieces left lying around are not only unsightly and can be easily damaged, but also offer homes for pests.

The activity of the compost bins slows down over the winter months, but continue collecting material and turning over the bins at regular intervals. It is more important to stay strictly to the rules of compost making in the winter as we are relying entirely upon correct stacking and turning to induce the necessary heat into the heap.

Continue cropping the vegetables still in the garden.

Spring (February, March, April, May)

This is the most time-consuming period in the garden. Now is the time when the foundations are laid for the main harvest from the garden and full advantage is taken of the planning carried out over the winter period so that the gardener can swing into action as soon as the conditions are right.

The season starts off with seed sowing, initially indoors. These seedlings will be transplanted into individual pots before being hardened off for planting outside as and when the weather conditions permit. Sowings of early crops in the greenhouse will be followed by outdoor sowings and by this time the season will be in full swing.

Remember, if you are going for early crops then some form of protection from the weather will be required. It is surprising how far into the year we can be and still experience sufficiently severe frosts to do considerable damage, even well into the month of May.

Crop protection brings the words 'cloche' and 'frames' to mind.

Cloches do have several advantages over frames; they are relatively cheap, extremely mobile, can be used to protect any crop in any part of the garden, and one set of cloches can be used continuously throughout the season, moved from crop to crop.

To be successful with cloches a little planning is required. There is no point in using cloching methods if you check the growth by planting out in cold soil. Place the cloches in position two to three weeks before required. This lets the soil warm up, and I also place the tray of plants under the cloche for a few days so that they become acclimatised to the conditions before being planted into the soil.

Conservation of moisture is of prime importance, so ensure the ground is wet before setting up the cloches. The organically rich soil will hold this moisture for a considerable time before the need for artificial watering will arise.

Just as a plan was required for laying out the cloches so one is needed for lifting. Do it gently to harden off the plants. Open the ends initially, but beware of through draughts, and cover the ends at nights. Follow this a few days later by completely lifting off the cloches, again covering at night, until you finally remove the cloches altogether.

The time has now arrived for extensive compost making. As the weather becomes warmer the activity inside the compost bins increases at an incredible rate, and very quickly the stockpile for the summer and autumn needs begins to build up. As the plants become established after planting out, mulching can begin to suppress the weeds. The winter compost should be in a condition to use, and grass cuttings are now available which make an excellent mulching material.

Continue cropping the vegetables available in the garden.

Summer (May, June, July, August)

Sowing and planting out will be carried out at regular intervals to give a continuous supply throughout the season, by successional and intercropping methods. Once the likelihood of frosts has passed then delicate crops such as runner beans can be sown and planted out.

On the whole this is the period to enjoy the fruits of your labour.

Harvesting will continue for these are the months of plenty; there should be so much available that one is spoilt for choice.

. Compost making and mulching will be a prominent activity. It is also essential to keep an eye on the weather for watering must be undertaken during dry periods. Do not leave it too late before taking action for once the soil has dried out it becomes more difficult to wet again, and do give enough water to penetrate down to the roots. A five-minute watering session will do more harm than good; it is better not to water at all than to do it incorrectly.

Keep an eye on pests and diseases and take action immediately. Once they become established, not only are they more difficult to cure but the isolated case may spread.

Along with your plants the weeds will be enjoying the rich ground and will compete for the available food. Keep them under control by laying down layers of newspaper with grass cuttings on top. Where it is not practical to do this then hoe or hand pick and remove them to the compost heap.

Autumn (August, September, October, November)

For the average gardener the season has come to a close, whereas we are still sowing to keep up our supplies. Spring cabbage needs to be sown, as well as a crop of the short-day type of lettuces for planting in the greenhouse to see us through the winter and early spring period. Window-sill gardening will come into its own with sprouting seeds, cress and corn salad grown in the house to supplement the salad bowl.

Harvesting of the summer-grown crops will continue and as the weather deteriorates storage will come to mind. I am a great believer in leaving the crops in the ground for as long as possible, using straw or Papronet for frost protection, as they keep very much better.

One very important point I must emphasise: if you are lifting crops in frost-attacked soil, *do not* turn in the frozen surface, but keep it on top. Once frost is buried it will take a great deal longer to thaw out and it is possible to find patches of buried frost when the top surface of the soil is clear. This leads to the ground remaining in a cold condition when we are looking for a fast warm-up to enable early crops to be planted out.

Spring cabbages should be sown and planted out before the ground becomes too cold to allow them to be established by the time winter is upon them. The same applies to autumn-sown broad beans. I then cover them with Papronet to keep off the worst of the weather and to give an early start to the season as spring approaches. One layer thickness is sufficient as these plants are hardy enough to stand the winter.

If green manuring is to be used in the rotation plan, this crop can be sown when the land is cleared. On the other plots as ground becomes vacant then mulching should be carried out as described in Chapter 2. Even small portions can be mulched and covered with folded polythene which, as more ground becomes vacant and mulched, can be unfolded to cover the newly mulched area.

Compost making should continue, but the decomposition activity is beginning to slow down as the weather grows colder. Keep collecting material and working the bins. As most of your summer-made compost will be used during this period of autumn mulching then every effort must be made to rebuild the stock for spring.

Successional sowing and intercropping

I have throughout the seasonal planning schedule used these terms in connection with maintaining continuous supplies of vegetables and full utilisation of the land, so let us now look at what they mean in more detail.

Successional cropping is the sowing or planting in vacant ground either before the main crop is grown or after it has been harvested. The term also includes the continual sowing or planting of a crop in its own bed to ensure a supply throughout the season. For example, lettuce can be planted out in March on ground allocated for a crop such as French beans to be sown or planted in May/June, or to follow the early cabbage, peas or potatoes as they are lifted in July/August, or it may be allocated its own bed with a few plants grown at a time to give a continuous supply.

Successional cropping uses the quick-maturing crops to give a fast 'in and out'. Some of these quick-maturing crops do not exhibit good keeping properties, so it is important to grow a little but often, especially in the early spring when the selection out of the garden is very limited. These young, tender plants are very refreshing after the winter. Successful successional cropping can be obtained with lettuce, radish, beetroot, carrots and onions.

Carrots and beetroot play a dual role for varieties are available for producing an early crop, the young roots being lifted as soon as they are large enough but, just as important, if left to reach maturity they produce a main crop for storing for winter use. Onions are similar; they can be lifted when small but may be left in the ground to grow to main-crop size for storing.

Intercropping is the growing of these quick-maturing crops between rows or even between the plants of those crops that take longer to reach maturity, although I would omit carrots and beetroot from this category. The brassica plot is an ideal area for intercropping as the spacing between each row and plant allows ample room for lettuces, radishes, spinach and onion sets, all of which will be of sufficient size for picking before the brassicas overshadow them.

I also grow broad beans in the brassica plot. They have the height to survive and are a bonus not only for the additional crop, but for their nitrogen-fixing nodules on the roots.

Do not forget the greenhouse where successional and inter-cropping can also be applied very effectively (see Chapter 7).

Crop rotation

The cropping plan must allow for crop rotation. As the term implies, the same crop should not be grown on the same piece of land two years running.

A garden of my size can be divided into three plots, the family of crops being moved round one plot each year so that a period of two years elapses before the crops return to the same area. In larger gardens a four-plot system can be operated where the families can be further divided, or one plot may be left vacant for green manuring. As I have said before, nature does not leave soil bare so it is better to cover it with a beneficial neutral crop rather than let it be covered with weeds. In either case a three-year cycle is operated.

Why is crop rotation so important? The primary reason is the prevention of the carry-over of pests and diseases, which can be built up to a very high level in the soil if a monocultural system is adopted. The majority of the pests and diseases are peculiar to one family only, so that the removal of this family from the area to be replaced by a non-affected family will break the cycle. However, some, such as club root, are very persistent, and I will deal with these under a separate heading.

Another important reason for rotating the crops is that different families require different soil conditions, and each plot can be prepared to give the optimum growing conditions. For example, brassicas prefer alkaline conditions, whereas potatoes prefer acid conditions. Some gardening books recommend that onions, for instance, should be grown in a specially prepared bed year after year, and if you grow a crop such as asparagus then this cannot be moved round the garden each year, so why not have an alkaline bed for brassicas and an acid bed for potatoes? But nature works in harmony with all things and keeps the garden in a state of equilibrium and if care is not exercised the balance within the soil can easily be upset. As discussed in Chapter 3 too much lime (I use the word in its broadest sense and do not mean the product purchased from the garden centre) will lock up valuable nutrients in the soil, so creating deficiencies, and will cause rapid exhaustion of the organic matter. By rotating the crops and treating the soil accordingly all this can be avoided, the natural balance being retained to maintain the soil in its peak condition.

Crop rotation also allows for the grouping of crops to enable sections of the land to be cleared for successional sowing, green manuring or the application of compost in preparation for the next season.

The crops can be split into compatible groups and the generally recognised groups for a three-year rotation are:

Roots	*Legumes and others*	*Brassicas*
Potatoes	Peas	Cabbage
Carrots	Beans	Brussels sprouts
Beetroot	Leeks	Cauliflower
Parsnips	Celery	Broccoli
Onions	Lettuce	Kale
		Savoy
		Swede
		Turnip
		Radish

Swedes, turnip and radish as members of the brassica family are susceptible to the diseases of that family. However, they are frequently found classified under the root group, a differentiation being made between the leaf brassicas and the root brassicas. Swedes, due to the length of their growing season, I include in the brassica plot rotation, but as turnips and radish are grown as successional crops, they fit in where space is available. This has no detrimental effects as they tend to be grown in the same area each year and follow the rotational cycle of that area.

For a four-year rotation, potatoes are allocated a group of their own. This is because the growing conditions of potatoes can vary dramatically from the other root crops, potatoes totally disliking alkaline conditions but enjoying very heavy manuring. The other root crops will fork if manure is applied; however, when the mulching techniques are used, both crops grow very happily together, and on page 126 I describe how to give potatoes individual treatment.

The leaf vegetables require a high nitrogen soil content and as the legumes are nitrogen providers then it is beneficial to organise the rotation sequence for the brassicas to follow the legumes.

The above lists are not complete, but cover the basic families to be grown in a small garden. If you wish to grow a variety not mentioned then it should be a fairly easy matter to allocate it to one of the groups.

I do not always stay rigidly to the groupings for in a small garden a certain amount of flexibility must be retained. However, one rule I do not break at any time is the strict rotation of the brassicas and potatoes as these two are more susceptible to disease than almost any other vegetable.

Space is at a premium in the small garden and if I stayed with the conventional recommended spacing, then I would crop considerably less than I do, even though each item would be individually larger. We are not looking for exhibition-quality produce; size is not important. In fact, I feel it is preferable to have a large number of small-sized products than a small number of large. The reason for this is that once a vegetable has been harvested it immediately starts to deteriorate, losing in particular its vitamin content, so the fresh vegetable not only has a better flavour but contains more of its goodness.

Consequently spacing can be very much reduced, and in fact I would describe my arrangement as squeezing the vegetables into the available area (staggering the plants in adjacent rows is a very useful ploy). Every square inch of ground must be productive, but to compensate for this heavy strain on the ground's resources it is of the utmost importance that I maintain a high level of fertility in the garden.

Although I have left this point to the end it is one of the most important statements in this chapter – always *keep a record*. Unless you have an exceptional memory you will find it impossible to remember detailed events from one year to the next. I keep two diaries, one a notebook allocating pages to each vegetable, listing only variety, dates of sowing, transplanting, planting out, first day of cropping, and a note on whether or not a variety is worth retaining for future years. The second is a diary where I record every detail of my daily gardening activities. As well as the above, I include compost mixes, fertiliser applications, poundage cropped, weather conditions, spacing of rows and plants and any other information I feel will be of use at a later date. It is surprising how often reference is made to each diary throughout the season.

It is important to keep a record not only to enable the selection to be made at seed-buying time, but so that you get to know your garden, what it can and cannot do. Do not be afraid to try new ideas and to adapt and modify existing practices to meet your needs. It may take a year or two to develop a technique fully and it is not always prudent to rely purely on memory, so – write it down.

Chapter Five

Tools for the job

Good tools are essential, so buy those of good quality and the best you can afford, for they will be in constant use and will be required to last a lifetime. Select carefully; just as you would try on a piece of clothing before buying, the same applies to the tools. Handle them in the shop, check their balance, imagine how they would feel with a load of compost or soil on the end. Could you work with them all day without feeling tired? Test them and visit different shops to look at various makes. You will be surprised how each varies, even the same item made by the same manufacturer. You will only buy once, so make sure it is the right choice for you before doing so.

Many tools now have stainless steel blades which give the added advantage of not rusting. Is it worth the extra expense? Mine are all of mild steel and all will last to the end of my gardening career. It is a poor gardener who does not look after his tools. Clean them after use, keep them in the shed out of the rain, and they can be handed down for generations. Wipe with an oily cloth before putting them away over the winter.

What do you need?

First on the list is the garden fork, the tool which will be used most of all in making and spreading compost and the lifting of the root crops. Next in order of usage comes the hand trowel for planting out. I have several, one kept permanently in the greenhouse and one in the shed for filling the paper pots with compost. If more than one person is working in the garden, you will need one each, otherwise the job will only proceed as fast as the one with the trowel. A hand fork is also very useful for lifting the weeds, so as not to leave any of the roots in the ground.

Despite adopting the no-dig method of gardening, a spade is also required for cleaning out the bottom of the compost bins, changing the soil in the greenhouse, and trenching out for peas, potatoes and the brassicas. An alternative to the spade is a trenching tool. There are a number on the market; I find the shield-shaped blade better than the flat edge.

You will also need a hoe and a rake as well as sundry items such as a garden line, dibber, secateurs and a good sharp knife, and no doubt you will accumulate other items as the years go on. A rack in the shed or garage will keep the tools in good condition and at a glance you will be able to select the one needed and see which have not been replaced at the end of the day.

Although not really a tool, but still a necessary item is a hose. Keep it on a reel; not only does this prevent damage, but makes it much easier to use. Some form of spray head will be needed as our objective is to copy the action of the rain. The spray can be either hand held or one of the proprietary rotating sprinklers can be used. On very few occasions will you use an open-ended hose – it is surprising the amount of damage it can do, washing plants out of the soil, or even snapping them off with the force of the water.

A watering can is an essential piece of equipment, especially in the greenhouse. Buy one of 9-litre (2-gal) capacity with the long spout, called a 'Haws' type, to enable the water to reach the corners of the greenhouse which are hidden behind foliage. They are made in both galvanised metal and plastic. The galvanised ones are very expensive, and the plastic ones are just as good for the amateur gardener. I have had mine for 15 years and it is still going strong.

A hand spray for foliar feeding and syringing the beans and tomatoes will be on the list. The days of the brass syringes are at an end and they are now almost impossible to buy, being replaced by plastic gadgets. A very useful one is the A S L 'Killaspray', a 2.5- or 4.5-litre (4 or 8-pint) plastic pot which is pressurised by a hand pump and gives a spray from a fine mist to a jet for up to several minutes before needing to be repressurised. (The offending words on the pot are easily rubbed off if you face ridicule from your non-organic gardening neighbours!)

You will also require a wheelbarrow. Select carefully, for it will see a great deal of use, bringing in the raw materials for compost making and moving compost about the garden. The choice is not easy, for many of the very lightweight barrows do not stand up to heavy wear and tear and do not give more than two to three years' use. They normally fail on the wheel bearings, which take all the load. On the other hand, the type with pneumatic tyres tends to be a bit on the heavy side and when full of compost it can be impossible for the slight person to move. A difficult choice, so have a chat with your fellow gardeners for their advice. You could have a look at the ball-wheel type or even consider a small truck if you find a barrow hard work.

Water requirements

Every day of the growing season water will be needed for some part of the garden, be it only for a pot or for the whole area. Bad watering can be more harmful than no water, so care must be taken in deciding when and how much.

The major water user is the greenhouse, and the most convenient source of this water is the greenhouse roof. Not only will it supply rainwater, free from the added chemicals of drinking water, but after sitting in a barrel all day, the water will have been warmed up by the sun. If you live in a dense industrialised area, rainwater can be highly contaminated by chimney pollution, so check the pH as described in Chapter 3. It is surprising how much water is used in the greenhouse; it takes only a few days without rain for the water level in the barrel to drop dramatically. The more you collect the better, but this requires storage space, which is always at a premium in the small garden. Run guttering along both sides of the greenhouse to feed one or two barrels – they can be joined together so access to one is all that is needed to draw off water. The shed roof is another good source of water.

Any container can be used as a collector, but ideally 182 litres (40 gal) is the minimum capacity. The container can be of plastic or metal, although metal drums do have the big disadvantage of rusting while the plastic purpose-made water butts are expensive. The barrel will need to be raised off the ground to allow the watering can or a bucket to be placed under the tap. Make a secure platform for a full barrel is heavy – 182 litres (40 gal) of water weighs 180 kg (400 lb).

The watering of large areas requires a hose and a convenient tap. If a water pipe can be run into the vegetable area so much the better, but more often a house tap is all that is available.

Make sure good tap connectors are used; a leaking connector or the hose blown off the tap by a loose one can leave quite a mess in the kitchen.

There are two common faults in watering. Firstly, it is often left too late, until the ground has dried out and is therefore difficult to re-wet. What then happens is that a 'pan' is created, which further watering will not penetrate, for the water simply runs off. The solution is to let the pan dry out a little, then to break up the crust with the hoe, taking care not to bring dry soil from underneath to the surface. Repeat this until the water has soaked into the dry layer. Heavy rain during a dry spell of weather or the use of an open-ended hose can also create a pan.

Secondly, sufficient water must be applied to penetrate deep into the soil where the roots are, somewhere in the region of 10 cm (4 in) deep. The bad practice of only watering the top layer encourages the roots to come to the surface, only to be scorched by the sun. During a normal summer, the soil can lose by evaporation (transpiration) between 1.75 to 3.4 litres (4 to 6 pints) per square metre (yard) per day and if there are long spells between rain this loss will need to be replaced. To ensure sufficient is being applied to penetrate to the roots, a small hole can be dug and the level of moisture in the soil examined. However, I find a much easier method is to take an empty jam jar, or some similar container, and using a waterproof pen, mark it every 1 cm (½ in) up from the bottom, and place it in the area being watered. Every centimetre (half inch) of water collected is equivalent to approximately 9 litres (2 gal) per square metre (yard). In this way if we are replenishing a week's loss, then 20 to 32 litres (4½ to 7 gal) per square metre (yard) is required or 32 to 45 mm (1¼ to 1¾ in) in the containers.

It is better to water in the early morning before the full heat of the sun is on the plants, and not in the evenings as is common practice. The reason for this is that as the evening cools down, the soil retains its heat, and to drench it with cold water destroys this overnight advantage, whereas when watered in the morning the soil will warm up again as the day progresses.

The same equally applies to the greenhouse: water in the early morning. I always keep a watering can full of water in the greenhouse, for in the event of an emergency I then have water at greenhouse temperature ready for use.

Whenever possible water seedtrays from the bottom by standing them in a tray of water or in the kitchen sink. This ensures the capillary action wets all the compost, for water applied to the top can run straight through without moistening the compost if it is on the dry side.

Cloches

Crop protection brings the word 'cloche' to mind and there are two types available on the market, glass and plastic or polythene. The glass types can be of either the plain tent or dutch barn design, both of which consist of sheets of glass supported on wire frames. They do have the advantage of letting more light through and it is possible to remove the odd pane of glass here and there for ventilation and hardening off. The disadvantages are that they are fairly expensive, the glass is easily broken and requires care when handling and storing for the winter. It also needs to be cleaned.

The plastic and polythene types again require wire frames, but this time the wires do not need any special forming so it is possible to make your own. Bent into a semi-circle and pushed into the ground a sufficient amount to offer rigidity, the plastic or polythene sheeting can be draped over them and the edges held down with bricks, wood or stones, or earthed up with soil to give a draughtproof covering. Being of simpler construction they are easier to store and depending upon your source the plastic or polythene sheeting may be discarded each year. The disadvantages are that the life of the items are much reduced, the material is affected by ultraviolet light, and the materials are more opaque than glass so the light to the plants is reduced. Care must therefore be taken not to allow the plants to become leggy, and ventilation is more troublesome. Both types have the disadvantage that as the plants are permanently under cover, watering is required, which may be a major task if the cloches have to be removed and then replaced to do this.

The Temple system

I have over the past years used a material called 'Papronet' as an alternative to the glass and plastic or polythene cloche. Papronet not only has all the advantages of plastic and polythene, with none of their disadvantages, but also being a very fine net material specially woven for use in crop protection, the mesh is sufficiently small to keep out the cold winds and the frost, but large enough to allow the cloche to breathe, letting in fresh air and the rain. The other advantage is that its use for this purpose was introduced by Jack Temple who has marketed the idea as the Temple System, which enables the less handy gardeners to purchase the net complete with all the framework to erect a good-sized cloche. It can also be used for bird, cat or dog protection, which is another requirement for cloches other than the weather, and also as protection against carrot fly damage (see page 149). Unfortunately Papronet is only available through mail order (see address on page 155). It is made in 1 m (3 ft) widths which are easily extended to 2 or 3 m (6 or 10 ft) by sewing lengths together using nylon thread. If looked after carefully, it will last for several years.

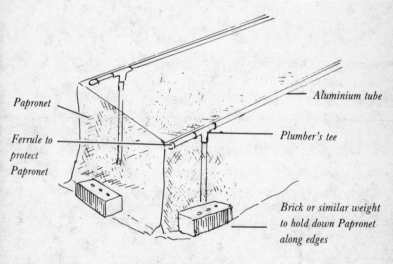

Papronet

Ferrule to protect Papronet

Aluminium tube

Plumber's tee

Brick or similar weight to hold down Papronet along edges

PAPRONET CLOCHE

I use a home-made version of the Temple system, comprising 1 cm (½ in) outside diameter aluminium tube, obtainable from any non-ferrous metal stockist, 15 mm end feed plumbers' tees, obtainable from your local plumbers' merchant, and 1 cm (½ in) bore plastic ferrules, obtainable from Coles Brothers Crawley Ltd, Stephenson Way, Crawley, West Sussex, RH10 1OF, (Part No. 10–31).

The aluminium tube is supplied in 5 m (16 ft) lengths and needs to be cut to make the vertical legs. Remember to add on the amount to be pushed into the soil when working out where to cut. Slide the copper tees on to the horizontal length and push them on to the vertical legs. Fit the ferrules over the ends of the tube to prevent any sharp edges ripping the Papronet. It is also a good idea to put ferrules on the legs, otherwise they will fill up with soil when being put in position. If building a fruit cage then cross-pieces will be needed at the ends, in which case 15 mm end feed elbows and corner tees will need to be added to the other items listed.

Chapter Six

Basic techniques

As you read the vegetable index in the seed catalogues you are faced with some 30 to 40 different varieties from which to choose. Some you will eliminate by personal choice, others for climatic reasons. However, a very common fault of the gardener cultivating a small area is to choose exotic or difficult-to-grow crops or even those which give a low return and at the end of the season the overall yield from the garden will have been poor.

In Chapter 4 I told you how to plan the garden and to do this effectively one must choose a very down-to-earth approach to the selection of vegetables and adopt the principle of supplying as much of your basic needs as possible. If you are unable to be self-sufficient then it is better to buy the odd luxury vegetable than those for your staple diet.

Consequently, I am restricting the vegetables described in Chapter 8 to those which I normally grow in my own small area and which give the best return for land used. The more land you have available then the more varieties you are able to grow, or you may prefer to grow more of one variety to give a supply throughout the year.

I split the seeds into two categories, those which are sown in seedtrays or pots then transplanted into their growing positions and those which are sown directly into the soil. The division is very simple; the only seeds I sow directly in the soil are those which cannot be transplanted, such as beetroot, carrots, parsnip, turnip and swede. Every other vegetable will be started in a pot or tray to be planted out when the conditions are right. The only exception is leeks, which although they can be started off in pots I find give better results if sown directly in the ground and then transplanted to their final position.

Sowing seed indoors

The method of seed sowing and handling in pots and trays is

similar for all varieties so I will discuss the basic techniques here, giving any individual treatment under the variety headings later.

Working in a small garden requires more planning than in the larger garden for space is at a premium. Ideally, we need to plant out at the earliest possible time not only to feed ourselves, but to leave sufficient time for a successional crop once the early crops have been lifted. Not only that but if we do have failures, and being honest we all have one now and again, then time is needed to re-sow. As a result early sowings will be started in the kitchen and then transferred to the greenhouse when the weather warms up.

Sowing dates will vary depending upon the part of the country you live in. The North can be as much as four to six weeks behind the South. The house sowing method will help in some respects for the northern gardeners to catch up on this delay.

All the seed I sow for transplanting starts off life in the same way. Fill an 8 cm (3 in) plastic pot with moist seed-sowing worm compost mix, firm it down to maintain the level at the step near the top of the pot, but do not cause compaction. Sow the seed thinly on top of the compost. Remember you may only be growing between five to twenty plants of any one variety and if you do this in two sowings for successional cropping you need no more than 12 to 15 seeds. Cover the seeds lightly. A common fault is to bury them too deeply when sowing. I believe a layer of compost the thickness of the seed is sufficient. The easiest way to do this is to take a fine-mesh sieve of say, 3 mm (⅛ in) mesh and as you shake it pass it once across the top of the pot. This will give the necessary covering. You would get away with not covering the seed at all but as the roots appear and go searching for the compost they are vulnerable to the outside elements and can be killed off by the heat of the sun.

The seedlings will tend to produce long roots, which can cause difficulties on pricking out. The length of root can be restricted by putting acid peat (Irish moss peat) in the bottom half of the pot. The roots will not grow into this medium but remain short, making it much easier to prick out.

Once the seed is sown place a label in the pot noting the crop and variety and the date of sowing. Also note these points in your diary. Cover the pot with a proprietary plastic pot propagator or small polythene bag held in place with an elastic band, to conserve warmth and moisture. Cling film can be used, but in this case hold the label in place with an elastic band round the pot. Place on the window-sill or staging in the greenhouse. Do not give any more water after sowing until the seeds have germinated.

When this has occurred, remove the covering to prevent the seedlings becoming leggy. Keep the compost moist by watering from the bottom of the pot. It is not good husbandry to water from the top: not only is there a tendency to wash the compost away from the roots at the point of impact, but also if the compost is dryish then it runs straight out of the bottom of the pot without wetting the contents. Sitting the pot in a tray of water and allowing the capillary action to do the work is the best and safest method.

If you have a number of pots on the go at once a good method is to use a houseplant window-sill tray. In the bottom of the tray place a mesh material of about 1 cm (½ in) thick or two pieces of 2.5 by 1-cm (1 by ½-in) wood, about 1 cm (½ in) apart, and put 5 mm (¼ in) of water in the tray. Take a 'Kerry wick' capillary stick and push it half into the plastic pot through one of the drainage holes, and bend the other half along the bottom of the pot. Place the pot on the mesh or the pieces of wood with the Kerry wick in the water. The bottom of the pot must be clear of the water. Water will now be sucked up the wick keeping the compost at the required moisture level. This is an ideal system if you have to leave the pots unattended for a period of time. Do not use wood which has been painted or treated with preservative.

Transplanting

The seedlings are ready for transplanting when they are large enough to handle, normally when the seed leaves have fully opened out. Do not leave them to grow too large at this stage.

Before starting to transplant prepare the potting-on medium and fill the appropriate pots or trays as described on page 76.

The handling of the seedlings at this stage in their life is very important. It is safer to empty the pot rather than dig out the seedlings. Do this by placing your first and second fingers across the top of the pot either side of the bunch of seedlings, taking care not to crush them between the fingers, grip the side of the pot with the thumb and third or fourth finger and turn the pot upside down. Now give the rim of the pot a gentle but firm tap on the edge of the bench, or table if working indoors, and the compost and seedlings will slide gently out of the pot to rest on your first two fingers. Remove the soil ball completely from the pot and lay it side down on the bench. Break up the compost with the dibber and the seedlings can now be picked up without any fear of damage to the roots. *Do not* handle the seedlings by the stem; this is one of the main causes of botrytis in seedlings. Always handle them by the leaves. If the compost is difficult to remove from the pot it is a sign that it is too dry, so give it a drink and try again a little later.

Dibber a hole in the potting compost making sure it is deep enough to allow the seedling to be inserted as close to the seed leaves as possible. Firm the soil around the roots but not so tightly as to cause compaction, then water, preferably from the bottom.

The reason for transplanting the seedlings as deeply as possible is that as the soil settles after watering it ensures there is still sufficient soil covering the roots. It also helps to encourage more root growth and keeps the stem short, preventing the plants from becoming top heavy and bending over during the early period of growth.

Note the date of transplanting on the label and place it with one of the seedlings. Also make a note in your diary together with any other points you feel may be of use at a later date.

Paper pots

The early part of the year sees the winter crops running out, but the weather still may be unsuitable to allow the early spring sowings outside, so in our efforts to be self-sufficient we must find a way to overcome the problems of bad weather conditions. This is simply done by sowing and growing as much as possible indoors. However, there are drawbacks for if care is not taken, we can end up with leggy plants; the growth is restricted and the plant becomes pot bound. The shock of transplanting can further check the growth, for if we wait for the weather to become suitable for planting then the plant may already be several weeks old.

The way round these difficulties is to use pots made from newspaper, for these have the advantages of being made to any shape and size, allowing the plant roots to grow through them with ease and, as with the mulching system, the paper rots after a time.

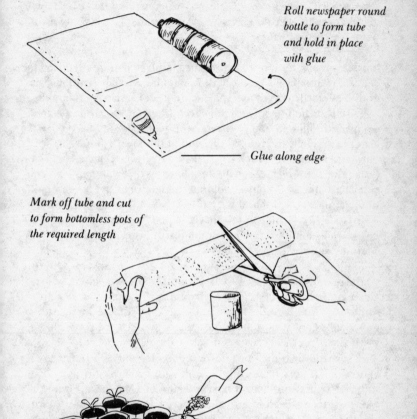

Roll newspaper round
bottle to form tube
and hold in place
with glue

——————— Glue along edge

Mark off tube and cut
to form bottomless pots of
the required length

Stand bottomless pots on end and
fill with soil – prick out seedlings,
one into each pot and label

MAKING PAPER POTS

75

Many gardeners use peat pots, but I find they are not so successful as the newspaper ones as they require careful watering. Peat, once it dries out, is difficult to wet again, and the roots do not grow through these pots as easily as newspaper, a very important point for early sowings.

Newspaper pots are very easy to make. All you need is an empty bottle – I use mainly two sizes of about 5 cm (2 in) and 9 cm (3½ in) diameter – a pair of scissors, a tube of paper or wood glue, and of course sheets of newspaper; the tabloid size is preferable.

Take a single opened-out full sheet, place the bottle on the long edge and roll into a tube, with a smear of glue along the edge to fix it in place. Hold the tube at one end and allow the bottle to slide out, remembering to catch it as it leaves the tube. If using the 5 cm (2 in) diameter bottle, cut the tube into eight equal lengths. You can easily mark this out by folding the length of the tube in half, then again and again and flatten to crease the folds. If using the 9 cm (3½ in) bottle, cut into six equal lengths, marking the positions by folding as before, but in thirds instead of halves. What could be simpler?

The next step is to take a standard 35 by 20 cm (14 by 8 in) seedtray and place one of the paper tubes on end in one corner. Drop enough potting worm mix compost in the tube to hold it round and stable and fill it about one third full. Add the other paper tubes one at a time in the same way until the tray is filled. With the 5 cm (2 in) diameter tubes the tray will hold 24 paper 'pots' and with the 9 cm (3½ in) diameter only 18 paper pots. When all the pots are in, fill them up with compost, firming down sufficiently to keep the compost level about 1 cm (½ in) from the top, but not so hard as to cause compaction. Place the trays in about 2.5 cm (an inch) of water to moisten the compost thoroughly, remove and drain off the excess water. The paper pots are now ready to take one seedling each.

As the seedlings grow the roots will fill the pots, and will easily penetrate the paper walls. This is the advantage of these pots when sowing early crops, for as the roots fill them, the seedlings can simply be transferred into a larger size of pot, the 5 cm (2 in) into the 9 cm (3½ in) and so on, without disturbing the rootball. This way the plant can be kept growing in the greenhouse or cold frame waiting for the appropriate weather for planting out. Even well-established plants can be transplanted without a check, since they are not removed from their pot as would be the case with plastic containers, but simply dropped into a hole in the ground, the roots growing through the paper which eventually rots. In this way seed sown indoors in February will happily grow until planted out as mature plants in late March to April, when the average gardener may only then be considering sowing seed.

Another advantage of this paper-pot method is economy of space. The trays can either hold 24 pots of one variety, or four pots of six varieties, or six pots of four varieties, and each one can be removed from the tray without disturbing its neighbour. Remember to label each variety to save mix-ups at a later date.

A proprietary system is the A P Propapack, a propagating pack consisting of expanded polystyrene slabs containing pot-shaped cells. The home-grower pack consists of slabs of two different sizes, six slabs of 24 cells, 5 cm (2 in) square, and six of 40 cells, 4 cm (1½ in) square. The slabs are washable and reusable and being of polystyrene keep the compost warm and promote growth. They can be used for sowing seed directly or for transplanting seedlings. With the special removal tool supplied the plants are popped out of the cells ready for planting out. Make a hardboard base for the slab to sit on. This prevents the compost falling out of the holes in the bottom and the roots from growing through and rooting in the soil. If this happens the roots will be torn when the slab is lifted, and plants with damaged roots never give a good crop.

I find them ideal for the main summer crops, particularly lettuce, where planting out begins as soon as the plants are large enough to handle. For the early sowings they suffer from the disadvantage of standard pots; if the plant is in for too long a period then growth is restricted.

Sowing in open ground

Having already made the point about not being able to make sufficient compost to mulch the whole of my area every year, it is this seedbed plot which is omitted as I am able to give these crops individual attention when seed sowing.

The setting out of the rows for these crops is very important for once the seed is sown very little can be done except to destroy the crop and start again, should you make a mistake. Use a line to mark out the row and measure the distance between rows exactly; every inch is important in the small garden and can very soon add up to the loss of a row.

Walk carefully down the line leaving an impression in the soil, remove the line and place pieces of cane or wood markers at the extreme ends of the imprint. Now reposition the line for the next row, measuring the exact spacing from the markers. Draw out a V-shaped drill carefully along the line impression using a hoe or trenching tool to a depth of 8 cm (3 in) by 10 cm (4 in) wide.

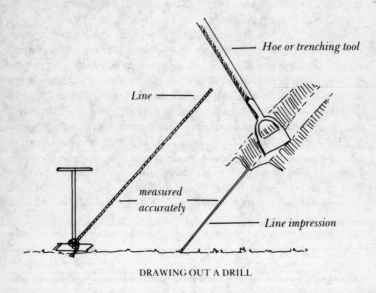

DRAWING OUT A DRILL

Fill the drill with worm compost potting mix, compressing it slightly, but do not compact it. Do this about a week before seed sowing to allow the rain to wet the compost thoroughly and any settling to take place before sowing. If settling does take place add more compost to raise the level again.

When ready to sow remove the row markers, replace the line and, using the hoe, draw out a drill to the required depth for the seed, sow and cover. When the seedlings are 5 to 8 cm (2 to 3 in) tall, dust the soil between the rows with 225 g (8 oz) per square metre (yard) of calcified seaweed, lay newspaper on top, four to five sheets thick, and cover with grass cuttings or compost, but take care not to bury the plants under the mulch.

Soil fertility from the worm compost and seaweed dressing, weed suppression and organic matter from the newspapers and grass cuttings give the seeds an ideal growing environment. The grass cuttings also allow you to walk between the rows, particularly during wet weather, without compacting the soil underneath. Keep replenishing the newspaper and grass cuttings at regular intervals.

Storage

Our requirement for vegetables is continuous over a 12-month period; unfortunately, however, the growing season for many is for a much shorter time. It is necessary therefore to store any excess produce.

Freezing is the best method for peas, beans, courgettes, cauliflower and tomatoes. Pick only vegetables in peak condition; do not use any that are past their best, and freeze immediately. Delay picking rather than leave them lying about. Use the open freezing method to retain their freshness, for blanching cooks them and much of the goodness ends up in the water, which inevitably is thrown away. The keeping life is reduced to six months.

Pod the peas and broad beans, cut the cauliflower (including calabrese) into pieces, slice the runners and French beans into 1 cm (½ in) lengths, cutting off ends and tips, cut the courgettes into 2.5 cm (1 in) slices and remove the seeds. Just cut tomatoes in half. Place on a tray and put in the fast-freeze compartment for one hour; remove and place in a freezer bag.

For the remaining crops, onions and potatoes apart, I find the best method is to overwinter them in the ground where they grow. Many are hardy and will surivive the winter without further attention, in fact I still believe the old saying that Brussels sprouts do not have a flavour until they have been frosted. The more delicate varieties such as carrots and beetroot require frost protection and this is easily achieved with Papronet. Earth up or use straw to cover the roots, then cover them with a double thickness of Papronet. No framework is required: just lay it on top of the foliage. Hold the Papronet down securely and just lift the roots when required. Use a double thickness as I have found that a single layer does not give adequate cover.

This method not only gives the necessary protection against frost damage, but also keeps the surrounding soil workable to enable these crops to be easily lifted with a fork.

I also use the straw mulch method on swedes, parsnips and leeks which, although they do not require any protection, are difficult, if not impossible, to lift when the ground is frozen. I have seen roots pulled in half when the ground has been too hard to use a fork.

Onions and potatoes both need to be lifted and dried before storing. The onions can be stored simply by laying them out in trays (the wooden tomato trays available from the greengrocer are ideal), or by stringing, which is the method I prefer.

To string onions take a piece of string about 1 m (3 ft) long and tie the ends together. Prepare the onions by ensuring they are dry, remove any soil left on the roots and loose skin on the bulb, keeping the leaves as long as possible. Hang the string by the knot from a hook in the wall or a door handle and pull tight. Thread the leaves of an onion through the bottom loop of the string to form a reef

Weave the first onion through the loop

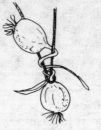
Make sure the weaving is tight and that the second onion rests on the first

Continue adding the onions, keeping the bunch balanced until it is about 40cm (15in) long

STRINGING ONIONS

80

knot. Take a second onion and thread the leaves through the legs of the string to form a figure 8 and pull down on to the first onion to keep the weaving tight. Repeat with a third onion, starting from the other side to keep the string balanced. Continue until the onions are about three quarters of the way up the string, then tie a knot in the string to make a loop to hang it up by.

An old pair of lady's tights is another way of storing, with the onions pushed down the legs. When ready to use simply cut off one toe, remove the onion and tie a knot in the tights to seal the hole. Keep undoing the knot until one leg is empty, then start on the other leg.

Keep the onions in a cool, dry, airy and frost-proof place and they will last well into the next year.

After the foliage of the main crop potatoes has died off, dig up the crop and leave on the ground for a few hours to dry. Remove any soil and examine the tubers for damage or disease. These tubers will not be stored, the damaged being used up first, the diseased being destroyed. Store in a hessian or paper sack; *do not* use polythene sacks for they will make the tubers sweat and rot. If sacks are not available stout cardboard boxes are a good alternative. Close over the opening to keep out the light, otherwise the tubers will turn green.

Keeping seed

I have mentioned that seeds can be kept for several years, so for the gardener who may only use a quarter to half a packet it is not necessary to buy fresh seed each year. All that happens is that germination falls off. The Ministry of Agriculture, Fisheries and Food in conjunction with the E.E.C. lay down minimum germination levels to which bought seed must conform. These vary from 25 per cent to 80 per cent, with most of those you will grow falling between 70 and 80 per cent. The older the seed then the poorer the germination, so in the second or third years sow the seed a little thicker to compensate for this. If you are unsure about the condition of the seed, a very simple check can be carried out. All you require is a saucer, pieces of absorbent material such as lint or blotting paper, 10 seeds, a maximum/minimum thermometer and a safe spot in the airing cupboard.

Moisten the absorbent material and place it in the saucer, count out the seeds and cover them with another piece of moist material, and place them in the airing cupboard. If you are checking more than one variety, remember to label them. Try to keep the seeds at a fairly uniform temperature, around 20°c (68°F) mark, but do not exceed 27°c (80°F). If the temperature drops it will only extend the germination period. Examine the seeds every day, keeping them moist; the time to germination will vary depending upon the variety, the faster seeds, such as radish, taking only one to two days, the slower seed, such as carrots, three to four weeks. At the end of the period count the number of seeds with roots, and this will give you the percentage of germination and tell you how thickly you need to sow the seeds to meet your needs. You can use the germinated seeds of the varieties which will transplant.

While on the subject of seed, some gardeners like to save their own seed and although I have nothing against this practice, I question the practicability of it for the small garden for several reasons.

1. Many of the new varieties appearing in the catalogues are labelled 'F1 hybrid' and these do not breed true unless cross-pollinated by the correct strain.

2. If you are growing more than one variety of a vegetable, remember that any cross pollination will not give a true strain, so allow only one variety to seed.

3. Beware of spreading disease, particularly with potatoes.

4. It does mean allowing plants to go to seed and there may not be sufficient room in the small garden for this.

However, if you really want to save your own seed, start off with peas and beans, which are very easy, and buy a copy of *Save Your Own Seed* from the Henry Doubleday Research Association (see page 154).

Length of time seed can be kept
(including year of purchase)

Beans (broad, French, runner)	3 years
Beetroot	3 years
Brassicas	5 years
Carrots	3 years

Celery	3 years
Courgettes	5 years
Cucumber	5 years
Leeks	3 years
Lettuce	1 year
Marrow	5 years
Parsnips	1 year
Peas	3 years
Radish	4 years
Spinach	2 years
Swede	3 years
Tomatoes	3 years
Turnip	2 years

Chapter Seven

Greenhouse and window-sill gardening

The greenhouse is a most essential piece of equipment in the vegetable garden, for its versatility will provide a home for the spring-sown seedlings and plants until they can be hardened off, and for the crops for harvesting in the early summer and over the cold winter months, as well as for raising the conventional summer crops. A garden without a greenhouse is limited in the variety of produce grown, with the gardener very reliant upon bought-in plants from the nursery or garden centre. I rate the need for a greenhouse so highly that if I had room for nothing else then that would fill the available space.

Choosing your greenhouse

It is a costly item and once in position is unlikely to be moved, so care is needed in both its selection and siting.

Choose the site first: it will have an influence on the size and type you select. Not only does a greenhouse offer shelter against the weather, it is also a suntrap, and the plants need the maximum amount of light. Beware of nearby trees and shrubs, for shadows cast in the winter are very much longer than in summer.

The majority of greenhouses are rectangular in shape so a decision has to be made whether to set it in a north to south or east to west position. The latter offers a large surface area of glass to the sun, which is of particular importance during the short daylight periods of the winter. However, during the hot summer days this effect can be a disadvantage for the temperatures can rise very high and good ventilation is needed to prevent overheating. But I feel that for 12-month cropping the advantage outweighs the disadvantage and I recommend the greenhouse is run from east to west with the door at the opposite end to the prevailing wind. If you are only interested in growing summer crops, then the north to south arrangement can be considered.

Access is an important factor. The greenhouse will be used a great deal throughout the year, and don't forget the wheelbarrow – if you decide to change the soil, sufficient room will be needed to get it in and out of the door. Access will be needed to all four sides of the greenhouse for maintenance and washing of the glass. No doubt a water barrel will be used to collect water from the roof so remember to allow room for drawing off this water.

There are three basic shapes to choose from: the Dutch light, the span roof, and the lean-to which is built against a house, garage or shed wall. The choice is one of personal preference to suit the site. A lean-to type does have an advantage of being very much warmer if one of the walls is of brick, for brick holds its heat well into the evening hours. Have you noticed how many of the older well-established gardens, particularly those of the houses open to the public, have the north wall of the greenhouse built of brick? It is important, of course, to build the greenhouse on the south side of the wall for there is insufficient light and sun if the north side of the wall is used.

Buy the biggest greenhouse you can fit in or can afford. What appears to be adequate at the time of choosing, somehow turns out to be far too small once you have mastered the techniques of cropping under glass. Just as you will never be able to make enough compost, so your greenhouse will never be big enough. Not only do you get more in a large greenhouse, but the temperature is also more stable, as the larger air volume does not respond so quickly to sudden fluctuations.

There is also a choice of material, wood or aluminium. Again personal preference will decide, for both types offer advantages. Wood tends to be warmer than aluminium, and it is also much easier to fix nails and screws to the frame for ties. The best wood is cedar or oak, which if correctly looked after will last a lifetime. However the wooden greenhouse does require a lot more maintenance than the aluminium one, needing a coat of preservative every year, or at least every three years. The greenhouse atmosphere will make the wood continually wet over long periods and green algae will grow, which will need to be removed.

Pests will enjoy the crevices of the joints of both types, so the greenhouse will need to be washed down regularly to clean the crevices and the glass. I do mine every spring and autumn.

Irrespective of construction material, the greenhouse should sit on foundation stones, normally supplied with the greenhouse and held down, for even the largest of greenhouses can move in gale force winds. Again pegs are normally supplied for pinning the frame to the foundation stones.

Staging
Staging is needed for laying out trays and pots. Unless you have an exceptionally large greenhouse, where you can afford the space, staging will only be needed temporarily over the spring period, so it should be capable of being easily erected in position and then dismantled when not in use. The laying of trays on the soil not only takes up valuable growing space but if there are bugs in the soil, they will soon find their way to the seedlings.

Ventilation
Good ventilation is a very important feature and unfortunately this is lacking in many greenhouses. Even quite large sizes are limited to two roof ventilators. No doubt this is linked to cost and strength of construction. Very few have side wall ventilators which are useful, for once the tomatoes and cucumbers are producing foliage the air is unable to circulate freely at ground level and stagnant pockets form. Stagnant areas are bad even in cold weather. It is better to be well ventilated than to close up the greenhouse in an attempt to keep it warm. However, you should avoid draughts and not confuse them with ventilation. An automatic ventilator is a very useful addition to the greenhouse, opening according to the atmospheric temperature inside and making life easier especially on those days when it is difficult to judge whether or not to ventilate.

It is an easy job to put in additional ventilation by removing a pane of glass and replacing it with a plastic panel fitted with a simple Vent-O-Matic type of fitting. My wooden greenhouse has a wooden panel in the door in which I have drilled eight 2 cm (¾ in) diameter holes on a 15 cm (6 in) diameter with a matching aluminium disc held to the wood by a nut and bolt. Turning the aluminium disc either covers or exposes the holes in the door, controlling the intake of air.

A maximum-minimum thermometer is another necessary item. It will record the lowest temperature at night and the highest during the day to help you regulate the conditions in the greenhouse.

Heating

Heating is always a topic for argument. I do not heat my greenhouse at any time of the year. I feel that the small benefit does not merit the cost of a reliable heater and the fuel bill. All that is required is to keep the greenhouse frost proof, one or two degrees above freezing point – 0°C (32°F). If there are delicate plants which need protection, then I will erect a cloche inside the greenhouse or cover them with Papronet, just enough to keep off the frost. Starting the seeds off in the kitchen does away with any need for heat for germination purposes.

Watering

All watering will be by artificial means, so a good readily available supply is needed, the water barrel being the most convenient. Some gardeners consider running a tap to supply both the greenhouse and the garden and this is generally a worthwhile venture. Water just sufficiently to keep the plants looking fresh. To overdo the watering and having the plants sitting in sodden compost is only inviting attack from disease. Less water is needed during cold weather. Judging the correct amount will become second nature with a little practice. During the hot summer days, sprinkle water on the greenhouse floor and windows and syringe the foliage to prevent the atmosphere becoming too dry and to take some of the heat out of the air. Keep the watering can full and stand it in the greenhouse at all times for this will give a supply of water at greenhouse temperature, which will avoid chilling the plants with cold water. Always water in the morning, not before going to bed, so that the plants are not left in the cold overnight.

Cropping plans

Many methods of growing produce in the greenhouse have been developed: ring culture, straw bales, and hydroponics, mostly based on the cultivation of one individual crop. Our aim is to utilise the area fully with a multiple crop arrangement, by growing directly in the soil, so that the needs of all plants are supplied. Garden compost and worm compost supplemented with the organic fertilisers applied between each cropping cycle and as a boost feed during the growing period will keep the soil healthy and fertile. Coupled with growing your own plants from seed, there should be no need to change the soil. If you have any doubts about soil health do not sterilise it, for this will destroy all the life in the soil, the good and the bad. It is better and safer to dig it out and replace with fresh. On the occasions I have changed the soil I have replaced it with 100 per cent compost to give an immediate high level of fertility, for my greenhouse is extensively cropped throughout the year.

The principles of garden hygiene and pest and disease control apply equally well to the greenhouse. Do not fill it up with dirty trays, boxes or pots, or leave rubbish lying about. Once established, pests can be very damaging and difficult to remove.

Planning in the greenhouse is just as important as for any other part of the garden, and I draw out three cropping plans to cover the year, each devised to maintain a continual output over the 12 months. Naturally there must be some overlapping, the majority of plants being quite happy to share ground during the early stages of their development. Divide the greenhouse into three plots and operate a crop rotation system, for exactly the same reasons as outside, for we are creating a mini garden under cover.

The cropping plans are only suggestions; for instance, cress may be grown in preference to lettuce over the winter, although I prefer to grow this in the kitchen and what could be nicer than new potatoes for Christmas Day from seed planted in the late summer?

Cultivation details are given for each individual crop in the next chapter, but the following can be used as a ready-reckoner.

Season	Crop	Sow	Plant
Autumn/	Celery	Late March	June
Winter	Leaf beet	June-July	August
	Spring cabbage	End of July – early August	Sept. – Oct.
	Lettuce	End of July – early October	August – Oct.
Spring	Beetroot	End of February	–
	Carrots	End of February	–
	Lettuce	January – February	Feb. – March
Summer	Tomatoes	Mid March	May
	Cucumber	Late April – early May	June
	Radish	March – May	–

GREENHOUSE CROPPING PLANS

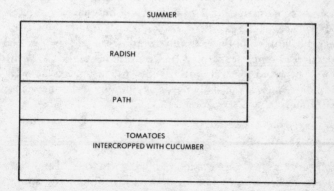

AUTUMN/WINTER

CELERY	LEAF BEET (SPINACH)	
PATH		SPRING CABBAGE
LETTUCE (SOW JULY/AUGUST)		

SPRING

LETTUCE (SOW JANUARY/FEBRUARY)	
PATH	SPRING CABBAGE
CARROTS & BEETROOT (SOW JANUARY/FEBRUARY)	

SUMMER

RADISH
PATH
TOMATOES INTERCROPPED WITH CUCUMBER

Frames

Plants raised in the greenhouse have to go through an intermediate stage before being planted in the ground, known as 'hardening off'. The purpose is to acclimatise them gradually to the colder, unprotected conditions out of doors. Failure to do so would chill the plants to the extent of affecting their growth, often referred to as a 'check'. The simple way to do this is by using a cold frame, like a mini greenhouse with a lid, which enables the plants to be enclosed and kept warm at night and kept out of draughts and protected from cold weather during the day. The extent of exposure is gradually increased until the plant is totally unprotected.

Frames come in all shapes and sizes. They do not necessarily need a permanent site, or need be of a rigid structure. A few planks of wood or bricks to form the walls and a sheet of glass for the roof is just as adequate. Alternatively cloches can be used.

Like the greenhouse, the frame should never stand idle. Courgettes, marrows, radish and lettuces are good crops for early spring and summer growing.

Window-sill cultivation

During the winter months the selection out of the garden is limited. There are the few hardy varieties of vegetables which will survive the cold winds, frosts and snow and the stored crops, but little else. In very short supply are the fresh greens for the salad plate, for although greenhouse lettuce can continue late into the year, even those become scarce during January and February.

However, one area where the conditions are ideal for growing over the winter months is a sunny window-sill and there is a large selection of crops which will thrive in these conditions with the bonus of requiring very little time and attention as well as providing most of our daily needs of vitamins and minerals to see us through the winter period.

Sprouting seeds

This is the largest source of food from the window-sill and you will find them listed in cookbooks under the other names, sprouting beans or sprouting grains, as the majority of the seeds fall into these categories.

Unlike today's vegetables they have a long history, for they were known to have been part of the diet in China as far back as 3000 B C. It was not until the eighteenth century that their importance came to the forefront in Britain when they were used in the diet of sailors at sea to prevent scurvy.

All are easy to grow, and are an ideal introduction to gardening for children, since they can watch the development of a plant from a seed producing a shoot and root without the mess of soil and in a short time span which suits the impatience of children. If purchased through a seed merchant, detailed cultivation instructions are printed on the packets. However, the same principle applies to all the seeds although one or two exhibit their own peculiarities, mainly in the length of time of germination.

How to grow them

The most common method is to use a glass jar. The size will vary depending upon the requirements. For an individual a 450-g (1-lb) honey jar will no doubt be big enough (a honey jar is of better proportions than a jam jar) whereas for the larger family a kilner jar is about the correct size. Any type of jar will do but choose one with a wide mouth; it is much easier to remove the sprouts through a large hole.

Place the dry seed in the jar and cover the mouth with a piece of muslin, a J-cloth or similar porous cloth, and hold it in position with an elastic band. Remember the seeds will grow between four to ten times their initial volume. One tablespoon per 450-g (1-lb) jar (half the quantity for alfalfa) and up to 3 tablespoons for the large jar is a good starting point. Fill the jar half full of water through the muslin, shake well, then drain it simply by turning the jar upside down. Leave it at an angle on the draining board for a few minutes to ensure all excess water is run off then place it on the window-sill. Rinse the seeds every morning and evening without removing the muslin and in a few days you will be enjoying a tasty addition to the salad plate. If a quick germination is required then soak the seeds in water for several hours until they swell.

Many books recommend growing the sprouts in the dark, but those grown this way do not produce any green. I also find if I hide them away in a cupboard I forget to rinse them, so if you do simply require the white shoots then put the jar in a brown paper bag and leave it on the window-sill.

The second method

An alternative is to use a specially designed sprouter as marketed by Ambig. It has the advantage of being more acceptable aesthetically, is much more compact and capable of growing up to three different seeds at the same time. Although it is relatively expensive it is sturdy and will last for many years. I have had mine four years with no signs of any deterioration to date. The growing method is the same as for the jar but made much simpler with this purpose-built appliance.

In no time at all a mini-production line can be established producing a large variety of sprouts for fresh salads or to be cooked as a vegetable. I harvest the crop when about 2.5 to 4 cm (1 to 1½ in) in length for all the seeds. The sprouts will keep for several days if removed from the sprouter and stored in the refrigerator in a polythene bag, but do not attempt to freeze them.

A number of suppliers sell packets of mixed seeds. I prefer to grow the individual seeds as I have found with the mixes that not all germinate together, making it difficult to pick one of the sprouted seeds while the others are still in seed form. Some beans take longer to sprout than others and these, such as adzuki, need soaking overnight to give them a good start.

All seeds can be obtained from your local health food shop, which can be anything up to ten times cheaper than buying from the seed merchant as you are not paying for the fancy packaging. The average seedsman limits his selection to alfalfa, mung beans, adzuki beans and fenugreek, so many are only available from the health food shop anyway. Two suppliers worth mentioning are Chase Seeds Ltd who offer these four seeds organically grown, and Thompson and Morgan, who offer a wide selection of the more uncommon sprouting seeds.

Remember that everything can be eaten, the sprout, seed and root.

What to grow?

Any dried whole bean or pea will germinate to give an edible sprout except runner and kidney beans, which are toxic unless boiled for ten minutes. These sprouted seeds are a good source of protein, vitamins, minerals and amino acids, with some being richer than others. I would recommend the following:

Alfalfa

As well as being the fastest growing it is also the richest of all the sprouting seeds containing 35 per cent protein, vitamins A, B complex including the rare B12, C, D, E, K, G and U with the minerals calcium, phosphorus, iron, potassium, magnesium and sodium – a meal on its own.

Mung beans

Also known as 'bean sprouts' in Chinese restaurants, these can be cooked (steamed or fried) as well as eaten raw. They contain 35 per cent protein with the vitamins B and C.

Adzuki

Again, these can be cooked as well as added to the salad bowl and have a very distinctive nutty flavour. They contain 25 per cent protein with vitamins B and C, but take several days longer to germinate than some of the other beans.

Fenugreek

Not as spicy as the smell would indicate, but they make a very tasty additive to soups and stews, with 25 per cent protein, vitamins A, D and C and iron.

Others to try are:

Lima beans	Navy beans
Soya beans (these must be cooked)	Barley
Chickpeas	Wheat
Lentils	Oats
Peas (garden)	Maize

Cress

The advantage of window-sill gardening lies in its simplicity and this is a real favourite with children. A family of seeds is so easy to grow yet supplies a valuable contribution to the diet.

Cress can be grown in almost anything: a flower pot or a castaway plastic container such as a margarine tub, or in a purpose-made unit similar to the Ambig seed raiser. The principle is identical no matter which one you use.

Fill the containers with damp potting compost to about 1 cm (½ in) from the top, sprinkle the seed fairly thickly on top but do not cover with compost. No real harm is done if you do cover the seed except that compost particles will stick to the cress as it grows and will have to be washed off before eating. The container now needs to be covered to encourage the correct environment for germination, and I find the easiest method is to wrap it in cling film. The Ambig unit is provided with its own lid.

The seeds will germinate inside two or three days and I leave the cling film in place until the leaves begin to touch it. When it is removed allow the growth to continue until the leaves open fully. This is the time to harvest the crop.

If growing in a flower pot or plastic container, do not allow the compost to dry out. The Ambig unit has the advantage of a water reservoir in the bottom with a capillary wick which maintains the compost at the correct moisture level.

The question of whether or not to grow it in the dark also arises with cress. I grow it in the light. It may take a day longer to germinate the seed, but life is made so much easier and once a systematic growing procedure has been established then an extra day is neither here nor there.

After cropping keep the compost moist and in two or three days a second crop will begin to grow, not as thick as the first but sufficient for another meal. You can of course mix the cress with the mustard, but remember to sow the cress three days before the mustard so that both will be ready at the same time.

My favourite variety of cress is 'Salad Rape'. It has long stems and the large leaf of the mustard but without the hot flavour. I find it keeps well and generally gives a better crop than the curly cress.

Corn salad

If you have any room left on the window-sill then a plant of corn salad is well worth growing. It gets its name as it grows wild in corn fields, although it is commonly referred to as 'lamb's lettuce' for it does resemble a lettuce in many respects.

Growing it is a little more complicated than the previously mentioned crops, for it is sown and grown as you would a lettuce, although this plant can be grown all the year round. Sow in March/April for an outdoor crop and for winter use sow in August/September. Put a pinch of seed in an 8 cm (3 in) pot in worm sowing compost, then lightly cover. When large enough to handle, transplant the individual seedlings into 5 cm (2 in) paper pots. When the plants are fully established transfer them into 13 cm (5 in) paper or plastic pots. All this can be carried out in the greenhouse, for at this time of the year there is still sufficient heat to keep them growing. Once the weather begins to cool bring the pots into the house.

Cropping can be done in two ways: the entire plant can be cut or a few leaves can be picked as required as you would with spinach. The more you pick the more it grows and you will have a supply of fresh greens for the winter months.

American or land cress can be grown in an identical manner. It has the taste and appearance of watercress.

Chapter Eight

Individual crops

Artichoke, Jerusalem

Unlike the globe variety, to which it is not related, this is a crop well worth considering for a small garden where it can be grown as a substitute for potatoes. It has lost its popularity in this age of convenience foods, probably due to its nobbly skin which makes it difficult to clean. I find its earthy taste very appealing, although not all would agree with me. It is capable of growing anywhere, not necessarily requiring its own bed, but fitting into odd corners, although the richer the ground then the better the crop. Being a member of the sunflower family it produces strong, tall growth, 2 to 3 m (6 to 10 ft) high, and is ideal for hiding the compost area if so required, nor is it out of place in the herbaceous border.

It is very similar to potatoes in habit and cultivation. The edible part is produced underground, grown from tubers retained from the previous year's crop. Select tubers about the size of a hen's egg and, starting early in March, plant 15 cm (6 in) deep with 30 cm (12 in) between tubers. If the tubers are large then simply cut them in half. As the foliage grows earth up as you would potatoes, applying comfrey foliar feed once a week. Do not allow them to dry out.

Harvest from October onwards, and although the crop can be lifted and stored in November, I prefer to overwinter artichokes in the ground. The tubers are hardy and will stand a moderate frost, but in severe frosts some protection will be needed. Always remember to save some tubers for next year's crop.

RECOMMENDED VARIETIES
Named varieties are not easily obtained these days and it is a case of using any tubers that are available.

SOWING AND HARVESTING GUIDE

Crop	Jan	Feb	Mar	Apr	May	June	July	Aug	Sept	Oct	Nov	Dec
Artichoke—Jerusalem			P							H	H	H
Beans—Broad		S	S/P	S/P	P	H	H	H	H			
—French				S	S	S/P	P/H	H	H	H		
—Runner				S	S	P	H	H	H			
Beetroot		Sg	S		S	S/Hg	S/Hg	H	H	H	H		
Broccoli—Sprouting		H	H	H/S	S	P	P					
—Calabrese				S	P		H	H				
Brussels sprouts	H	H	H/S	S/P	P						H	H
Cabbage—Spring		H	H	H	H		S	S	P	P		
—Summer		S	S/P	S/P	P/H	H	H	H	H			
—Winter	H	H		S	S/P	P	P			H	H	H
Capsicum			S	S	P	P		H	H			
Carrots		Sg	S	S	S/Hg	S/Hg	H	H	H	H		
Cauliflower—Summer			S	P			H	H	H			
—Autumn	H	H	H	S	S/P	P	P			H	H	H
—Winter	H	H	H	S	S/P	P	P			H	H	H
Celery	H		S	S	P	P			H	H	H	H
Cucumber					S	P	H	H	H			
Garlic				P	P					H		
Leeks	H	H	H	H/S		P	P		H	H	H	H
Lettuce—Spring	Sg	Sg		Hg	Hg	Hg						
—Summer			S	S	S/H	S/H	S/H	H	H	H		
—Winter	Hg	Hg	Hg					Sg	Sg	Sg	Hg	Hg
Marrow				S	S	P	H	H	H			
Onion—Seed	S	S		P			H	H	H			
—Sets		P	P				H	H	H			
Parsnips	H	H	H	H/S	H/S				H	H	H	H
Peas			P	P	P	P/H	H	H	H	H		
Potato			P	P		H	H	H	H	H		
Radish			S	S/H	S/H	S/H	S/H	S/H	H			
Rhubarb	H	H	H	H	H	H	H					
Spinach	H	H	H/S	H/S	S/H	S/H	S/H	S/H	S/H	H	H	H
Spinach beet				S	S	S	S/H	H	H	H	H	H
Swede	H	H	H		S					H	H	H
Tomato		S	S	P	P	H	H	H	H			
Turnip					S	S	S/H	H	H	H	H	

Code: Sow—S   Plant out—P   Harvest—H

Sow for greenhouse crop—Sg   Harvest greenhouse crop—Hg

Beetroot

Can be used on the salad plate either raw or boiled or served hot as a main-course vegetable.

The first sowing is an early variety in the greenhouse in mid-February, to give a crop by the end of May. Prepare the soil by dosing with 225 g (8 oz) per square metre (yard) of calcified seaweed, followed by a 5 cm (2 in) layer of well-rotted compost. Sow in rows 1 cm (½ in) deep and 15 cm (6 in) apart. The seeds are large enough to be easily spaced out to two every 2.5 cm (1 in). This is thicker than an outdoor sowing as the weather can still be very cold and the germination failure rate high. Cover the seed with worm compost potting mix, which gives more control over the depth to which the seed will be buried than would be achieved if the rough compost was used.

To give the seeds the best possible start, cover the soil with a double thickness of Papronet as soon as the border has been prepared, and replace the Papronet immediately after sowing. This will keep the soil warm. If the soil looks dry, water about a week before sowing, but use water which has been stored in the greenhouse, otherwise considerable heat losses will occur in the soil if icy cold water out of the water barrel is used. Leave the Papronet in place until germination takes place, then remove it gradually, leaving it off during the day and replacing it at night until the little seedlings have been fully hardened off.

Leave thinning until the roots are large enough to eat – about the size of a golf ball – then remove every second and third as and when required, leaving the remaining roots to mature. Plan ahead, for there will be a clash for space with the tomatoes. Using canes, mark out the positions for the tomatoes and harvest the beetroot to create a space of 25 cm (10 in) in diameter around the cane. This gives ample clearance for the tomatoes. Do not allow the soil to dry out.

Take care when lifting beetroot for any damage to the roots or skin will cause 'bleeding'. When removing the top, do not cut it but simply hold in both hands and twist it off about 5 to 8 cm (2 to 3 in) above the crown.

These early roots I recommend be used raw and grated either directly on to the salad plate or in coleslaws. They are so refreshing after the stored crops, I feel it is a shame to detract from their flavour by cooking.

The outdoor sowing should be started in mid-April and continued till June. Sow half a row at a time to give a succession of roots from July onwards. Prepare the drills as described (see page 78) and sow the seeds one every 2.5 cm (1 in), 2.5 cm (1 in) deep with 23 cm (9 in) between rows. When the seedlings are about 2.5 cm (1 in) high, lay down the seaweed, newspaper and grass-cutting mulch between the rows and apart from watering in dry weather, the beetroot will require very little attention. Thin out when the roots are large enough for table use.

I find two 6 m (20 ft) rows adequate, one of an early variety and one a main crop. A packet of seed will sow one row.

Beetroot are best stored in their growing position (see page 79), for unless carefully lifted and stored in sand or peat they will turn soft very quickly. The roots can also be boiled and pickled for safe keeping.

RECOMMENDED VARIETIES   *Early* – Boltardy (Round)
                                                – Regala (Round)
                   Main crop – Detroit (Round)
                                                – Cheltenham Green Top (Long)
                                                 – Cylindra (Long)

Broad beans

One of the hardiest and earliest of the vegetables, giving a heavy yield with the minimum of attention.

Sowing can begin indoors in early February, one seed to a 9 cm (3½ in) paper pot on the kitchen window-sill. If space is short on the window-sill, then put three seeds in a 10 cm (4 in) plastic pot and transplant into individual paper pots once germinated. Push the seed end on into the compost to a depth of 5 cm (2 in). Once the weather warms up a little, in mid-March, transfer the plants to the greenhouse, but with all changes of environment do it gradually. Repeat the sowings every three weeks into May to ensure a continuous crop until September. The later sowings can be made in the greenhouse, or directly in the soil from the end of March onwards, but I prefer to use the paper pots throughout to prevent gaps in the row.

Chitting the seeds before planting not only speeds up germination, but as a germinated seed is being sown the likelihood of the
seed failing to grow into a plant is very much reduced. Details of
chitting is the same as for peas (see page 123).

Plant out in ground mulched the previous autumn. Trowel out a
hole and drop in the paper pot, leaving about 1 cm (½ in) of pot
above the soil surface as a protection against slugs. If you have
been unable to mulch, then trench out as for sowing seed in the
ground and fill in the trench with worm compost potting mix after
planting.

Protect the early plants with cloches or a Papronet tent, having
put these in position a few weeks earlier to warm up the soil. Plant
out 15 cm (6 in) between plants and 23 cm (9 in) between rows,
staggering the plants for a double row with 45 cm (18 in) between
the double rows. Broad beans can also be intercropped between
the cabbages. The tall varieties will need staking to prevent wind
damage, otherwise the root structure will be weakened, leading to
attack from pests and diseases. Apart from this and the laying
down of the seaweed, newspaper and grass-cutting mulch and a
foliar feed with liquid comfrey, the beans need very little attention.

Harvest as soon as the pods are full and the beans are about the
size of a new penny. Start picking from the bottom of the plant,
taking a few pods from each plant at a time to encourage the rest to
develop. Any excess can be frozen for use later in the year. The tops
may also be pinched out and used as a green vegetable.

When lifting the plants at the end of the season, cut the stems off
at ground level and leave the roots behind to allow the nitrogen-
fixing nodules to release this nitrogen into the soil.

RECOMMENDED VARIETIES   *Dwarf* – The Sutton
                                        – Bonny Lad
                             Tall – Dreadnought
                                        – Masterpiece
                                        – Aquadulce
                                        – Express

French beans

Treat as for broad beans, starting off with individual seeds in paper
pots, but as they are not as hardy the sowings must be left till later
in the year. The early sowing should not be made before mid-April

and will continue every two weeks till June. These sowings can be made in the greenhouse. Outdoor sowings should be left until the first week in May.

French beans enjoy rich soil, so this is one of the areas which should be treated with an autumn compost mulch. Keep them growing fast throughout the season by watering frequently during dry weather and using the newspaper and grass-cutting mulch to preserve the moisture in the soil and keep the plants clear of weeds.

Plant out in late May in double rows 23 cm (9 in) between plants and 30 cm (12 in) between the rows and stagger the plants in each row. If more than one double row is planted, then about 53 to 60 cm (21 to 24 in) between double rows is needed to give access for harvesting. When planting out the paper pots, again leave 1 cm (½ in) above soil level for slug protection. As the flowers appear, to help setting, spray in the evenings with tepid water. This is best obtained by leaving a can in the greenhouse to warm up. Use a syringe, not a hose. Do not use cold water out of the tap as the sudden shock of being chilled can lead to bud drop. Foliar feed with comfrey liquid throughout the growing period.

Start picking when the beans are 8 to 10 cm (3 to 4 in) long. Letting them grow too long or coarse will restrict the production of the beans still to come as well as losing some of the flavour.

RECOMMENDED VARIETIES   Prince
                             Masterpiece

Runner beans

Runner beans are one of the most popular vegetables, giving a very high return for the amount of land used and effort required. There are very few gardens or allotments where the lines of scarlet flowers are not seen. As for the French beans, rich soil will give the best results, so the area should be given an autumn mulch. However, the runner bean will grow practically anywhere and produce an acceptable crop. I have read of a bean grown in a pot on a patio and trained up the house which gave a very good crop.

The runner bean, however, is very tender and the young plants are easily killed off by frost, so sowing should be begun in the last week of April in the greenhouse. Again, I use the paper pot method and as with all the beans the seeds are pushed end on into the compost to a depth of 5 cm (2 in). For an outdoor sowing the earliest date is the first week of May. Chitting the seeds (see peas) helps to prevent gaps in the rows, but is not a guarantee as seeds do rot, and irrespective of which method is used, it is a good idea always to keep a few plants in case of emergencies, for frosts can go on into June in some areas.

Hardening off the greenhouse sowings should be begun in the last week of May in readiness for planting out in the first week of June. As the plants require staking it is better to position these before planting to prevent any damage to the roots when pushing the stakes into the ground. Unless you have a good source of hazel bean poles, use garden canes. I use 2.5 m (8 ft) long canes in two rows to form a wigwam support, pushing the canes well into the ground vertically, pulling them to the centre and securing them tightly at the top to a horizontal cane running the length of the row. The height of the wigwam is governed by the practicalities of cropping. Remember that you have to reach the top to pick the beans. The fully grown beans will offer a tremendous barrier to the wind, so make sure that they are well staked. There is nothing more disappointing than to find a beautiful crop lying ruined on

Runner bean wigwam support

Shoots trained horizontally round wigwam supports

RUNNER BEAN SUPPORT

the ground through careless staking. The canes should be placed 23 cm (9 in) apart with 45 cm (18 in) between the rows. For added strength in windy areas additional horizontal canes may be used halfway between the soil and the top of the canes.

In the small garden the wigwam may be of only four or six canes and such an arrangement is certainly not out of place in the flower border, for these plants are themselves beautiful with their mass of scarlet flowers covered with bees.

Plant out using the paper pot procedure and water the soil well, for the beans do not like dry conditions, and mulch to preserve the moisture in the soil. Continue to water throughout the summer, wetting the soil and not the leaves. An overhead spray is beneficial during hot, dry spells. Do this during the day and not the evening, and keep a good mulch around the stems. Spray the flowers to help them set as for the French beans, remembering to use tepid water. Foliar feed once a week with liquid comfrey.

As the plant grows it will curl itself up the stakes till it reaches the top, at which point the growing tip should be pinched out. However, if you only have room for the four to six cane arrangement, then the crop will be limited to the 2 m (6 ft) of beans for each cane. This can be increased by training the bean horizontally instead of upwards. When the stem has grown about 60 cm (24 in) long, very gently untwist about 38 cm (15 in) and take the stem over to the adjacent cane, retwisting the growing tip around this cane. Do this with all the plants and continue training the beans round the canes in this manner at 15 cm (6 in) intervals. It can be seen that the length of the bean plant has thus been extended from 2 m (6 ft) to many times this figure.

The beans should be picked young and not allowed to grow too long or coarse, giving those unpleasant strings which are difficult to chew. The more you pick the more beans will come on.

If the plants suffer from an attack of blackfly or red spider mite, give a boost feed of undiluted worm compost, lightly forked into the soil, and increase the frequency of foliar feeding to three times a week. As the red spider mite is particularly active during hot, dry spells, overhead spraying of clear water during these periods will minimise the chances of attack.

RECOMMENDED VARIETIES   Prizewinner
Streamline
Scarlet Emperor
Red Knight

Brassicas

Under this family heading I will be covering broccoli, cauliflower, cabbage, Brussels sprouts and savoy. All are liable to attack from club root and cabbage root fly and as a consequence all should receive the same ground preparation and treatment.

This family needs a rich, firm soil with a pH of 6.5 to 7.5 and as a consequence the plot should be treated in the autumn with 225 g (8 oz) per square metre (yard) of dolomite to correct the pH balance. Remember, if in doubt check the pH level as described in Chapter 3. Ground limestone at the same rate is just as effective, but I like the additional magnesium of the dolomite. Follow this with 225 g (8 oz) per square metre (yard) of seaweed meal and 55 g (2 oz) per square metre (yard) of Alginure. Lay down the newspapers or cardboard with a 10 cm (4 in) layer of compost on top, and cover with black polythene sheeting for the winter.

Seeds can be sown in 8 cm (3 in) plastic pots, being transferred to paper pots for continuous growing, hardened off, and then planted out. Individual treatment will be discussed under each heading.

When the time is right for planting out, remove the polythene sheeting. Only remove enough to meet your immediate planting programme, and leave the rest of the ground under cover to keep warm. Mark out the row with a line, adopting the same techniques as for growing in the soil, and gently walk down the line so that its impression is left in the soil. Remove the line and place it at the next row, but remember to position it accurately. Using a hoe or trenching tool, take out a V-shaped trench 10 to 15 cm (4 to 6 in) deep.

Trowel out a hole 5 cm (2 in) deep at each planting position, again measuring these carefully to make sure your planned quota is laid out. Drop in a paper pot complete with plant, and earth up firmly, using worm compost potting mix, to within about 1 cm (½ in) from the top of the paper. By doing this you will be combating the root fly, club root and slugs all at the same time. As the plant grows, slowly fill in the trench with New Zealand bin compost together with 225 g (8 oz) of calcified seaweed per 9-litre (2-gal) bucketful, adding compost around the roots until the stem is earthed up. Do not worry about all the walking up and down this will entail for it helps to create the firm, well-consolidated bed liked by brassicas. If the rain shows signs of running off, just hoe the top inch to conserve the moisture. But if your soil is very heavy, then lay down a board for walking up and down; the ground only needs to be firm, not compacted.

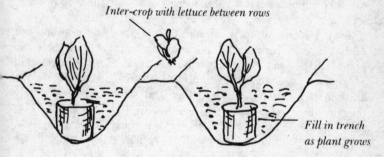

Inter-crop with lettuce between rows

Fill in trench as plant grows

PLANTING OUT BRASSICAS

Brassicas enjoy a lot of room which the small garden does not have. Some allowance can be made for this by staggering the plants in adjacent rows to give that extra inch or two. Do not at any time allow the plants to dry out, particularly during the early stages. The trench is of value in this respect, for it can be filled with water to ensure the roots are kept moist.

Birds have a tendency to peck the newly planted out brassicas, so protect the young plants with Papronet.

Broccoli

This can be a confusing family for the name covers a number of types – heading broccoli, often referred to as winter cauliflower, sprouting broccoli and calabrese. The heading broccoli is very similar in cultivation to cauliflower, so I will concentrate on the sprouting broccoli and calabrese.

Sprouting broccoli

As its name suggests, a number of sprouting shoots are produced with a cauliflower curd at the end. It is a valuable vegetable, for being very hardy it will withstand the extreme winter weather of any part of the country. From February/March onwards, when there is little else left in the garden, it will provide a profusion of shoots over a period of weeks, giving a maximum return for the space occupied. It does have one big disadvantage for the small garden, for it is in the ground for up to 12 months and requires careful positioning if it is not to cause havoc with the crop rotation schemes.

Sowing starts in April through to mid-May and planting out takes place in June and July, allowing 60 cm (24 in) between plants and 45 cm (18 in) between rows. As they are relatively tall plants staking is advisable to prevent them blowing over in the autumn and winter winds. The shoots should be cut immediately the curds are well developed, when they are 10 to 15 cm (4 to 6 in) long but before any flower buds begin to open showing a yellow colour. The profusion of shoots will necessitate daily cutting. Some protection may be needed as the crop is liable to attack from pigeons who look upon it as a delicacy.

RECOMMENDED VARIETIES   Early Purple Sprouting
                          Late Purple Sprouting

Calabrese

This gives a centre head similar to a cauliflower. When this is cut off the plant will produce shoots similar to the sprouting broccoli, but smaller in size (known as broccoli spears). These shoots are cut off when about 10 to 15 cm (4 to 6 in) long.

Sow in April for transplanting during May, allowing 60 cm (24 in) between plants and 45 cm (18 in) between rows. The crop will be ready to harvest from the end of July onwards. Keep cutting and more spears will develop. Do not allow the spears to open into flowers. Cook and serve like asparagus.

RECOMMENDED VARIETIES   Corvet (late variety)
                          Green Comet (early variety)
                          Green Sprouting

Brussels sprouts

One of the most popular vegetables for the winter period and the most useful, as cropping can be continued for a considerable period. Seeds are sown from mid-March to April. Planting out is done in April/May, allowing 60 cm (24 in) between plants and 53 cm (21 in) between rows. Being tall plants, they require to be staked to prevent them being blown over. They like firm soil – any loosening of the roots and the plant will fail to form tight buttons. Instead, the sprouts will open out into a bunch of individual leaves. A shortage of potash coupled with excess nitrogen can also cause this effect.

Start picking the sprouts from the bottom, working up the stem to the top. Leave the top to develop, for it can be cut off and used as a green vegetable. If you go from one plant to another, removing the bottom sprouts and working up the stem as the sprouts develop, you will get a continuous yield over a period.

RECOMMENDED VARIETIES   Achilles (Dobies)
Peer Gynt
Citadel

Cabbage

With a little planning this vegetable can be available throughout the year by using three groups of cabbage – the spring cabbage, the early quick-maturing summer variety and the slower-maturing variety for the autumn and winter.

The summer and autumn varieties are sown from late February through to March for the early summer group and up to May for the winter varieties. Planting out will begin in April for the early varieties and continue up to July for the winter kinds. Allow 30 cm (12 in) between plants and 38 cm (15 in) between rows.

Spring cabbages are sown at the end of July to mid-August, and planted out in their final positions in September to early October. Planting of this variety can be in the greenhouse or cold frame, which gives protection over the cold weather and an earlier crop. Succession can be extended with another row outside.

RECOMMENDED VARIETIES *Summer* – Hispi
– Minicole
– Golden Acre
Autumn/Winter – Celtic
– Christmas Drumhead
– Winningstadt
Spring – Myatts Early Offenham
– Offenham Flowers of Spring

Savoy

This is really just another variety of cabbage but is extremely hardy, surviving the winter to produce heads for cutting from January to April. Savoys are recognised by their crinkled leaves in contrast to the smooth leaves of a standard cabbage.

Cultivation is identical to that for cabbage, with seed sown from the end of April to about mid-May.

RECOMMENDED VARIETIES January King
Ormskirk Late

Capsicum (Sweet pepper)

The sweet pepper is increasing in popularity both for the salad bowl and as a cooked dish. There is no difference between the green and the red except that the red has been allowed to ripen on the plant. They are very easy to grow and may be planted outside, in the greenhouse or simply in a large pot and placed on a south-facing window-sill.

Sow the seeds in 8 cm (3 in) plastic pots in early March, pricking them out into 5 cm (2 in) paper pots as soon as they are large enough to handle. If planting them out of doors wait until the danger of any frosts has passed. A sheltered, sunny, south-facing spot is preferred. If growing in the greenhouse plant out during early May. A distance of 30 cm (12 in) between plants is sufficient.

Very little further attention is needed apart from ensuring that the plants do not dry out. They benefit from a daily syringe and a foliar feed twice a week. Each plant will then produce a succession of fruit over several months, which you can either pick green or leave to ripen.

RECOMMENDED VARIETIES   Canape
                                        Twiggy

Carrots

The early crop is obtained in the greenhouse from sowings made in mid-February. Soil preparation should be begun immediately the previous crop is lifted by an application of 225 g (8 oz) per square metre (yard) of calcified seaweed followed by a 5 cm (2 in) thick layer of well-rotted compost. Sow thinly, in rows 5 mm (¼ in) deep and 15 cm (6 in) apart, covering the seed with worm compost potting mix which gives more control over the covering process than using the ordinary compost.

Cover with a double thickness of Papronet as soon as the border has been prepared, to build up warmth in the soil. Do not allow the soil to dry out. About one week before sowing moisten with water which is at greenhouse temperature, otherwise the soil will be chilled and germination slowed down. Replace the Papronet after sowing and leave it until germination has taken place, when it can be removed during the day and replaced at night until the seedlings have been hardened off. The carrots will clash with the planting out of the tomatoes so mark out the position for the tomatoes with canes, then crop around these until an area has been cleared (about 25 cm [10 in] diameter is sufficient), to allow the tomatoes to be planted out. The tomatoes and carrots will grow very happily together.

Do not thin out but allow the carrots to grow until they are large enough to use, then pull the largest first and leave the rest to gain size. For these early sowings use a stump-rooted variety. Do not allow the soil to dry out at any time during their growth.

Providing the soil is not too wet or cold, the outdoor sowings can be started in mid-March and continued every three to four weeks up to July, for a successional crop. Prepare the rows as described on page 78, then sow 5 mm (¼ in) deep in rows 23 cm (9 in) apart. Sow very thinly; it is best if thinning at a later stage can be avoided, for this is when the carrot fly is encouraged. If thinning is needed do so on a dull evening, when the soil is moist and the plants are still young, firming the soil with the fingers around the roots left. Collect all thinnings and put them in the compost bin. If the sowing is thin enough, leave until the roots are large enough to eat then pull out for use until those remaining are 10 cm (4 in) apart. These roots are left for storing. I normally sow four rows, two of an early variety (which I do not thin) and two main crop.

Immediately sowing has taken place the rows should be covered with Papronet for protection against carrot fly and great care taken to ensure that the Papronet is always correctly in place and is not damaged or holed when being handled during harvesting. Once the carrots are established lay down the calcified seaweed, newspaper and grass-cutting mulch.

I prefer to store the carrots in their growing position (see page 79).

RECOMMENDED VARIETIES

Greenhouse –	Amsterdam Forcing
–	Rondo (Unwins)
Early outside –	Nantes Express
–	Chantenay Red Cored
Main crop –	James Scarlet Intermediate
–	Autumn King

Cauliflower

This is one of the most difficult vegetables to grow for the slightest check during the growing period will cause the head to bolt and run to seed before a good-sized curd has been formed. They are gross feeders, requiring very rich soil, and care must be taken to ensure that the seedlings are hardened off properly to prevent them being chilled on planting out. Do not allow them to dry out at any stage of their growth.

The cauliflower can be divided into three groups: summer, autumn (Australian varieties) and winter (heading broccoli). Cauliflowers must be cut immediately the curds are a good size, for if left too long they will turn to seed, so it is important to make a succession of sowings to avoid all the heads being ready together.

Start sowing in March for the summer varieties, leaving the Australian and winter ones till April or early May. Transplant before the plants become too big from April to June. Disturb the roots as little as possible when moving them and ensure they are firmly anchored in the soil. The paper-pot method will help with this procedure. Plant them out 60 cm (24 in) between plants with 45 cm (18 in) between rows.

Once the curds begin to form, break some of the leaves over them to protect them from the light, which tends to turn the curd an off-white yellow colour. On the winter varieties the breaking over of the leaves also helps to protect the curds against frost.

RECOMMENDED VARIETIES   *Early* – All The Year Round
                        – Early Snowball
            Autumn – Canberra (Australia)
                        – Mill Leaf (Australia)
                        – Veitches Autumn Giant
            Winter – English Winter Leamington

Celery

A very useful autumn and winter salad vegetable which is not too easy to grow. It needs a rich, moist, open soil and I find the best results are given by a greenhouse-grown crop.

The seeds are very small so it is best not to cover them when sowing but simply firm them into the compost with a flat piece of wood or similar implement. Sow in a seed raiser or plastic pot on the kitchen window-sill from mid-March to mid-April and prick out when large enough to handle into paper pots or the 5 cm (2 in) square polystyrene Propapacks and transfer them to the green-house.

After lifting the spring lettuce, apply calcified seaweed at a rate of 225 g (8 oz) per square metre (yard) followed by a 5 cm (2 in) layer of compost to the greenhouse border in preparation for planting out the celery plants in May. Leave 15 cm (6 in) between each plant and each row, staggering the plants in adjacent rows.

Celery is a hungry feeder, so a mulch of worm compost should be applied when the plants are 10 to 15 cm (4 to 6 in) tall. Keep well watered in dry weather, otherwise they will tend to go to seed.

The self-blanching or American green types are best for the greenhouse and will be ready for use from August onwards. They are not, however, very hardy. Covering with Papronet will give some protection but a severe frost can do considerable damage. Do not lift the plants should this happen, for they will grow again in the spring, producing young shoots from mid-March onwards.

For an outdoor crop the treatment is the same as for the greenhouse with seed sowing and transplanting into paper pots or the Propapack trays. As they are greedy plants, the ground needs to be treated with 225 g (8 oz) per square metre (yard) of calcified seaweed followed by a 5 cm (2 in) layer of well-rotted compost three or four weeks before planting out. The plants should be spaced 15 cm (6 in) apart with 23 cm (9 in) between rows from mid-May to the end of June. Watering is very important when growing outside for the plants must not be allowed to dry out at any time. A mulch of worm compost applied as for the greenhouse crop will ensure steady growth.

Again, I like to grow the self-blanching type but if a blanching variety is preferred earthing up should be started when the plants are fully grown, from mid-August to October depending upon the sowing dates. Earthing up before the plants have matured only restricts further growth. Remove any side growths from the base, wrap a piece of brown paper around the stems to form a collar and hold it in position with a piece of strong string. This prevents the soil getting into the heart as well as excluding the light. Now draw the soil up around the plants. It will take about six weeks to blanch the plants properly.

RECOMMENDED VARIETIES   *Self-blanching* – American Green
    – Golden Self-blanching
    Blanching – Giant White
    – Giant Pink

Cucumber

Although cucumbers can be grown outside they are much more successful under glass and will grow happily together with the tomatoes.

Select an all-female flower variety for it is not desirable that the female flowers should be fertilised, and with varieties that produce blooms of both sexes the male flowers need to be picked off as soon as they can be recognised. Failure to do this will result in the production of fruit which will taste very bitter and be unuseable. When grown in a small greenhouse, with the mass of foliage from both cucumbers and tomatoes, it is only too easy to miss a male flower and spoil the crop.

Sow two seeds in an 8 cm (3 in) pot, placing the seed end on and leaving the tip just showing out of the compost. This prevents the seeds rotting. Soaking the seeds overnight before sowing helps to speed up germination. Prick out into 5 cm (2 in) diameter paper pots when large enough to handle. Cucumbers need a minimum temperature of 18.5°C (65°F), so do not be in too much of a hurrry; the first week in May is early enough for sowing.

The same applies to planting out: the greenhouse soil needs to be at least 18.5°C (65°F), so leave it until early June. Plant deeply, just leaving the seed leaves above the soil, and water freely with water at greenhouse temperature. The cucumber is a surface-rooting plant and very soon these roots will be seen on the top of the soil. Mulch with a layer of chopped comfrey leaves followed by a 5 cm (2 in) layer of half-rotted worm compost. Two or three such dressings can be given over the season.

Cucumbers do not like direct sunlight. I find that growing them behind a row of tomatoes gives adequate protection. Spray the leaves during dry spells to prevent scorching.

The main stem will need to be staked or trained. Pinch it out when it reaches just short of the greenhouse roof. Side shoots will develop which can be trained along wires tied horizontally across the greenhouse. Pinch each out at two leaves past the first fruit, and also pinch out all tendrils. Secondary side shoots will appear from the first which will also bear fruit and these too should be pinched out at the second leaf. As the plants are cropped some of the older growth is cut out to encourage young shoots to develop. In this way a succession of fruit can be picked throughout the summer.

Cucumbers need more water than tomatoes, so selective watering needs to be carried out when mixed with tomatoes.

RECOMMENDED VARIETIES Fertila (all female)
Pepinex 69 (all female)
Monique (all female)
Petita (all female but may produce the occasional male flower)

Herbs

No garden is complete without a selection of herbs to dress the salad plate or flavour the main dish. They do not necessarily need their own bed for many are very attractive displayed in the flower border and a number can be effectively used as an edging plant. The simplest way to start is to buy a plant from the garden centre, but if a number of each plant is required then it is much cheaper to sow seed or take a cutting or a root division from a colleague's plant.

Some are annuals which need to be re-sown each year and I have had considerable success simply by allowing the plants to self-seed. If you have any doubts about this method then it is safer to sow new seed.

Take care in choosing their site, for herbs like a sunny position and a rich organic soil. For convenience for the cook in the household they should be positioned as close to the kitchen door as possible. Dress the ground with 225 g (8 oz) per square metre (yard) of calcified seaweed followed by a 5 cm (2 in) layer of compost three or four weeks before planting out. For the perennials a repeat dressing in the early spring will keep the ground fertile and the plants healthy.

For use over the winter months the herbs are best kept dried. Pick them on a warm sunny day and hang them up in bunches in a cool, airy place. When perfectly dry rub them between your hands into flakes and store in a jar. Parsley can be frozen but in this condition it is not really suitable for use raw in salads or as a garnish.

The selection of herbs available is almost endless and your choice will be to suit your own tastes so I will only discuss the most popular varieties. I am not going into any great detail for herbs can be used in many ways for cooking, herbal medicine or for companion planting. Each one is really a book on its own, all of which are available from your local library, bookshop or even the health food shop.

Balm

Due to its lemon scent it is commonly referred to as 'lemon balm'. An easy-to-grow perennial, the young leaves make a refreshing addition to the salad bowl or they can be cooked as a flavouring for the main dish. The leaves are also used in the preparation of herbal teas and because of their pleasant smell are very popular for use in pot-pourri.

Seeds are sown in April or May and the plants set out in their final position about 30 cm (12 in) apart. It can also be increased by root division in March or early September.

Borage

An annual which with its beautiful blue flowers is certainly not out of place in a flower border. It will seed freely in July and is one of the safest to allow to self-seed for next year's plants.

The leaves, which have a cucumber flavour, can be cooked like spinach or along with the flowers can be eaten raw in salads. They are also used in preparing cool, refreshing drinks or in the form of an infusion in hot water make a herbal remedy for sore throats.

Chives

Chives are a small perennial onion but in this case the leaves are eaten and not the bulb. Seeds are sown in March to April and thinned out to 23 cm (9 in) to allow for expansion or the plants can be increased by the splitting of an existing clump.

Cropping is simply by cutting the leaves off about 2.5 cm (1 in) above ground level. Finely chopped up they are excellent used in salads, sandwiches or as fillings in omelettes.

Chives can be very successfully grown over the winter period in a pot on the kitchen window-sill.

Garlic

This is a very easy-to-grow ingredient for the kitchen. Split the clove up into its separate bulbs and push them upright into the soil with the tips just below ground level. Planting is done from mid-March up to May. Just leave them – they need no further attention. Harvest as for onions, lifting and drying them before storing in a dry, cool, frost-proof place.

There are no varieties. Cloves can be obtained at your local greengrocer's or supermarket.

Mint

Better known as 'garden mint' or 'spearmint', it gives that unmistakeable smell when the leaves are rubbed between the fingers. A very valuable and necessary herb for the kitchen with a multitude of uses, the most famous of which is the sauce served with roast lamb.

For use, cut as required but if drying for storage, harvest in July. Do not pick after rain for if the leaves are wet they will not dry but turn mouldy.

A plant can be bought from the garden centre or obtained by root division in March. The growth may be a little slow the first year but do not be misled for if care is not taken the plant will take over in the garden in the following years. As a consequence it must be planted in a container to restrict its growth – a bucket or old washing bowl is ideal. Make a few holes in the bottom for drainage, otherwise the soil will become sour. When the container becomes overcrowded lift the plants in March and split the roots.

Parsley

The most popular of all the herbs and one which will be required all the year round. Although it is a perennial, the best results are gained by treating it as an annual and sowing seed every year. Ideally three sowings are needed to obtain a fresh supply, one in March, a second in May and then again in early August. The seeds are slow to germinate, taking as long as four or five weeks, and they must be kept moist during dry weather. The plant will re-seed itself if the seeds are allowed to develop, but this does weaken the growth of the main plant. Thin out the seedlings to 15 cm (6 in) apart.

Parsley has a number of uses, garnishing main-course dishes, adding to soups, salads and of course for making sauces. Parsley also makes an excellent edging plant for the border.

Rosemary

This perennial can grow up to 1.5 m (5 ft) tall if allowed to do so. It has the advantage that it will tolerate dry, sandy soil, but it does not like cold winds. It is easily grown from seed in March or from a cutting taken just after the plant has flowered. Set the plants out 1 m (3 ft) apart.

Rosemary is used extensively for flavouring meat dishes and is a popular companion plant for the control of the cabbage white butterfly in the brassica plot. It can be dried for winter use, when the leaves should be picked in August.

Sage

Along with parsley and mint, sage is the next most popular of the herbs although the flavour is very much stronger than the other two. It is a perennial of shrub habit which will grow into a very attractive bush about 1 m (3 ft) high.

It is best grown from cuttings of young growth taken in August or from seed sown in late April. Plants should be set out in their final positions about 60 cm (24 in) apart. For drying, cut in late June just before the plants come into flower.

The main use for sage is in the preparation of stuffing combined with onions.

Thyme

A dwarf perennial which makes a very attractive edging plant and is also ideally suited for the rockery. It can be raised from seed or by root division in April or by cuttings taken in July. Space the plants out to about 15 cm (6 in) apart.

Thyme can be picked all year round but for drying this is best carried out in June. To encourage new growth for the spring the plants should be cut right down in the autumn. Thyme likes alkaline soil and will benefit from a dressing of dolomite in the autumn.

Combined with parsley, it is used to make a stuffing for poultry or the leaves and flowers can be chopped and sprinkled on salad and meat dishes. It is also used in soups and stews.

Leeks

Despite having a long growing season leeks are well worth the space, not only for their flavour but also for their extreme hardiness. They will survive the winter weather and provide a crop from August through to the following May.

Although leeks can be started off in pots in the greenhouse, I prefer to sow them directly in the soil, from early April onwards. As the seedlings will be lifted and transplanted in June or July, in the small garden the sowing can be squeezed into the space between other crops, such as between the two rows of beetroot. Care, however, must be exercised when lifting them not to damage the beetroot. Sow the seeds 1 cm (½ in) deep.

In my garden leeks are a successional crop following the early potatoes. If you do have room to give them their own bed then naturally this is much better. To transplant, dibber a hole 15 to 23 cm (6 to 9 in) deep about 4 to 5 cm (1½ to 2 in) in diameter. Space out 15 cm (6 in) between holes in staggered rows 15 cm (6 in) apart. Lift the seedlings and drop one into each hole. If the leaves do not show above the top of the hole, do not worry, no harm will come to the plant. Do not fill in the hole with soil but instead fill it with water; this will wash sufficient soil down the hole to cover the roots and will allow room for the stem to swell as it develops. In this way the leeks are encouraged to grow a long stem, the portion in the ground being blanched, but remember that the green leaves contain as much food value as the white stem and should be eaten as well.

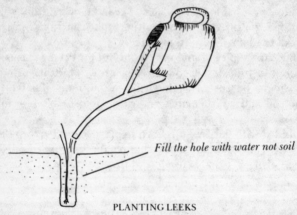

Fill the hole with water not soil

PLANTING LEEKS

Being hardy, there are no problems over storing leeks. Just lift and eat them when required. It is better to cover the ground with straw during frosty weather to allow a fork to penetrate for lifting.

RECOMMENDED VARIETIES   Musselburgh
Lyon
Cobham Improved

Lettuce

With a little care, lettuces can be available throughout the year, the outdoor varieties from May till October, the greenhouse varieties filling in the months between.

The secret of growing lettuces over the winter months is to choose a variety specifically bred for the colder, short-light days, understandably called 'short-day varieties'. Even so these varieties are still very weather dependent, for a long period of very cold weather will retard the crop. A fair amount of skill is needed to grow them successfully and the beginner will find difficulty in maintaining a crop during the January and February months. However, after a few seasons when experience has been gained on such items as when to water, or rather when *not* to water, and the use of cloches in the greenhouse for added protection, lettuces will be available throughout the year.

The use of summer lettuce over the winter period will not produce heads, but simply a few large outer leaves. The summer lettuces come in two types, the 'cabbage' with its round, solid head and the 'cos', with its long, oval-shaped leaves. The choice is entirely personal; both are of excellent flavour, both require the same culture.

The secret of raising successful lettuces is to keep them growing without any checks, particularly avoiding drying out, and although they will tolerate a certain amount of shade, an open, sunny position is preferred. No matter what variety or time of year, I start all lettuces off with a pinch of seed in an 8 cm (3 in) pot on the kitchen window-sill during the cold weather or in the greenhouse in the summer. Prick out into the Propapack trays and when large enough harden off and plant out. I do not allocate any space for lettuces, simply intercropping them between the brassicas and using any other areas where a lettuce can be popped in. In this way I can crop between 300 to 350 lettuces a year.

Apart from watering them well during dry weather, the summer lettuce requires very little attention.

RECOMMENDED VARIETIES

Early March Sowing – Reskia (J. W. Boyce)
April to June – Little Gem (cos)

- Webb's Wonderful
- Tom Thumb
- Winter Density (cos). Despite its
  name, it is also a very good summer lettuce
  going well into the winter
  months outside

July/August — Avondefiance
August — Ambassador (J. W. Boyce)
September/October — Delta (Asmer, Johnstons)
January/February — Ambassador

Marrow

One of my first memories of gardening as a child was the enormous marrows grown by my father and the hours the family spent making marrow and ginger jam. These days the popularity of marrows has been overtaken by the courgette, a member of the same family.

Both varieties are very tender and easily killed off by frost, so sowing is left till late April or the first week of May. Sow two seeds in an 8 cm (3 in) pot, with the seeds edge on just showing out of the compost to reduce the possibility of rotting. The seeds can be soaked beforehand for 24 hours to speed up germination. When large enough to handle, prick out into 6.5 cm (2½ in) diameter paper pots.

Water freely during the early stages of development and plant out in mid-June. I grow them in the cold frame for it has the advantage of giving protection should there be any likelihood of frost. Continue watering in dry weather.

Marrows enjoy a rich soil, so mulch with half-rotted worm compost or garden compost at least twice during the growing season. Before building a cold frame I used one of the New Zealand bins, growing them on top of the half-rotted compost, with great success. I obtained some of the best crops I have ever grown. The disadvantage was that the bin was out of action for compost-making purposes for a number of months.

The plant will produce both male and female flowers. The female needs to be fertilised by removing the petals from the male flower and pushing the pollen-covered stamen into the female. Use the male flower only once.

Male flower   *Female flower*

*Remove petals from male
flower and mate with female*

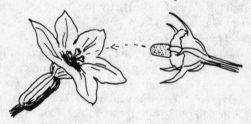

FERTILISING MARROW FLOWERS

Harvest before the fruit becomes old. Courgettes should be picked when 10 to 15 cm (4 to 6 in) long, and the marrows from about 30 cm (12 in) long. They should still feel a little soft when pressed at the blossom end. Marrows can be left to grow to full size if they are to be used for jam or for storing over the winter in a cool, dry place. They can also be frozen if cut into 2.5 cm (1 in) thick slices, cored and quick frozen – excellent for ratatouille.

RECOMMENDED VARIETIES   *Courgette* – All Green Bush
                                  Marrow – Zucchini

Onions

Onions can be produced in two different ways, either from seed sown indoors then transplanted to their growing position at a later date, or from sets. Onions like rich soil and the bed should be dosed in the autumn with 225 g (8 oz) per square metre (yard) of seaweed meal and 55 g (2 oz) per square metre (yard) of Alginure then covered with the cardboard, newspaper and compost mulch. Before planting out I like to hoe in a further 225 g (8 oz) per square metre (yard) of calcified seaweed.

Seed sowing can be started as early as mid-January, and is best done in a tray for the number to be grown will be too many for a pot. Cover the seed very thinly, then wrap in cling film and maintain at a temperature of about 10 to 13°C (50 to 55°F). Remove the cling film once the seeds have germinated. When about 5 cm (2 in) high, prick out the seedlings into paper pots or Propapack trays for planting out in mid-April. Plant out with the base of the stem just under the soil level in pairs of staggered rows, 15 cm (6 in) between plants and 15 cm (6 in) between rows, with each pair of rows 30 cm (12 in) apart.

Sets are by far the easier method of growing and it is the method I prefer. Sets are small onions partially grown the previous year, which when planted out will produce mature bulbs. Planting out starts in mid-March at the same spacing as for the seedlings. Push each set into the soil until the tip just shows above the surface. It would appear to be a favourite pastime of the birds to pull them up. If this is the case the sets can be buried completely, but it entails more work in drawing out drills. They can also be started off in boxes in the greenhouse and planted out when roots have developed. These roots are sufficient to hold the sets in place against the birds. This method also has the advantage of allowing the sets to be started off from mid-February, for those few early bulbs. Between each pair of rows lay down the newspaper and grass-cutting mulch to help to suppress any weeds.

The onions need little further attention until they are ready to harvest. If during the growing season an onion starts to produce a flower head, lift and use it straight away for the bulb will not develop any further. Towards the end of August bend over the leaves just above bulb level, and two weeks later loosen all the bulbs in the soil by placing a fork underneath and gently easing them slightly out of the ground. This will stop any growth and encourage ripening. After another two weeks lift them completely out of the ground and spread them out to dry. If the weather is wet, keep them in the greenhouse or in a cold frame. When completely dry, the leaves will have died off and the stem will feel dry when pressed. The onions can then be strung as described on page 80 and stored for use over the winter.

RECOMMENDED VARIETIES   *Seed* – Bedfordshire Champion
                            Sets – Sturon
                                   – Stuttgarter Giant

Parsnips

Another of the winter-hardy vegetables and in the small garden it is a choice between them and swedes for a root vegetable in the early part of the year.

Parsnips require a long growing season and therefore need to be sown in late March to early April. Sow in drills, prepared as described on page 78, 2.5 cm (1 in) deep with 30 cm (12 in) between the rows. The seeds are relatively large, allowing two to three seeds to be placed out every 10 cm (4 in). Thin out to the strongest seedling. Mulch either side of the rows with 225 g (8 oz) of calcified seaweed per square metre (yard), and with newspaper and grass cuttings, leaving the roots until ready for use from September through to April.

RECOMMENDED VARIETIES   White Gem
                            Offenham

Peas

One of the best-known and most popular of vegetables, peas are a favourite with my family, being eaten raw long before reaching the kitchen. Unless the weather conditions are just right, peas can be poor germinators; gaps in the row are the tell-tale signs of sowing when the soil is too cold or wet. Mice can also be troublesome, eating the seed, but on the whole, weather is the primary cause of poor germination.

I overcome the problem by 'chitting' the peas before sowing, that is, starting off germination in the greenhouse. Place a few sheets of damp newspaper in a seedtray, lay the pea seeds on top, then cover with another few sheets of damp newspaper. Keep damp at all times by pouring water over the top at least once a day.

The peas will swell and in about a week produce a root. At this stage they are ready for sowing; any not germinated may be left until they do. If the weather conditions are not suitable, do not rush to plant them out. I have on occasions been forced to wait, by which time the root has been 5 cm (2 in) long and leaves have been produced, but there has been no detrimental effect to the crop.

Preferably I like to grow the peas in an area mulched with compost the previous autumn, digging out a trench 5 cm (2 in) deep by a spade's width. Lay the chitted peas 5 cm (2 in) apart along the outer edges of the trench, then cover them, even if the peas have started to produce leaves – they will soon grow through. When filling in the trench leave a small depression along the centre. This will help to channel water to the roots, especially if watering is required during dry weather. Peas benefit from copious watering, especially when the pods are filling.

If you are unable to grow them on mulched land, dose the trench with 225 g (8 oz) of calcified seaweed per square metre (yard) before sowing, hoe in and fill in the trench with the worm compost potting mix.

Allow 53 cm (21 in) between rows (in a really small garden this may go down to 45 cm [18 in], but access between the rows for picking is much reduced). Once the peas are through sufficiently to define the rows, apply between the rows 225 g (8 oz) of calcified seaweed per square metre (yard), then cover with newspaper and grass cuttings. Repeat this twice during the season.

Peas are divided into early, second early and maincrop varieties, and can also be of dwarf or tall-growing habit. The differences between the varieties are the yield, maincrop giving a heavier yield than the earlies, and the length of time to maturity, earlies taking 10 to 12 weeks, maincrop 14 to 16 weeks. This helps you to plan a succession of peas throughout the season, for it is quite possible to sow an early variety late in the year to get a catch crop before the weather becomes too cold. Start in mid-March with an early sowing, followed by a second two weeks later, the main crop in mid-April and again two weeks later. If you have the space try another sowing of an early variety in the first week of June.

I recommend staking for all varieties, even the dwarf, some of which are only 30 to 45 cm (12 to 18 in) tall. If not staked they tend to fall over, making it difficult to pick the peas underneath and covering the path between rows, and I find the crop is greatly reduced. The main crop must be staked. Pea sticks (hazel branches) are best if they can be obtained, but failing that use netting. My method is to use a number of stakes to support the netting along the whole length of the row as follows. Screw a large hook into each 2.5 cm (1 in) square by 122 cm (48 in) long stake about 5 cm (2 in) from the top, then push the other end well into the ground working down the centre of a row, for they will have to hold the considerable weight of the peas as well as resist the wind. Take an aluminium tube, or garden canes joined together in lengths long enough to reach the hooks on the stakes, feed them through the netting and then support them on the hooks. Hold the netting in place at the bottom to prevent it blowing in the wind. The single length of netting makes picking very much easier and if the peas tend to grow away, simply thread a tendril through the net.

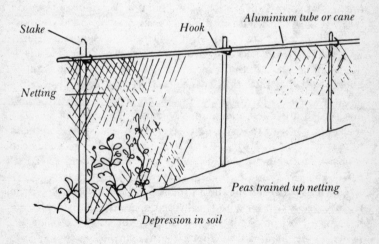

STAKING PEAS

Pick as soon as the pod is full, and do so regularly. This not only encourages the plants to go on producing but the flavour is completely lost once the peas are past their best. Any excess can be frozen for use later in the year.

RECOMMENDED VARIETIES *Early* – Little Marvel
– Kelvedon Wonder
Maincrop – Hurst Green Shaft
– Onward

Potatoes

Potatoes will produce a reasonable crop on even the poorest of soils, and are used for breaking in virgin land, but naturally, to obtain the best results good fertile soil is needed.

In the small garden the potato does not give a good return for the land used, and many recommend that the small-garden owner leaves out potatoes from his plans. I cannot resist the flavour of a new potato the size of a hen's egg, boiled then covered with a little butter, and so to get good land utilisation I grow the potatoes in pots.

The previous autumn prepare the ground by applying 225 g (8 oz) of seaweed meal plus 55 g (2 oz) of Alginure per square metre (yard), cover with cardboard or newspaper, and as compost is usually scarce I cover this with well-rotted horse manure, then with the polythene sheeting. The pots need to be 30 cm (12 in) in diameter and a minimum of 25 cm (10 in) high. They can be bought as whalehide pots, which are very expensive, or home made out of black polythene sheet, cut into strips of the correct size and turned into open-ended pots by joining the ends with either a freezer bag sealing machine or a series of staples. As the polythene tube is not self-supporting a stiff sleeve is needed to go inside the tube during the initial stage of filling. Only one of these is needed, as you move it from pot to pot as you work down the row.

The seed tubers should be purchased as early as possible. Place them in trays end on with their eyes uppermost and store in the light in a frost-proof place to sprout. By the time the seeds are ready to be planted out short, sturdy purplish-green looking sprouts will have been produced. Planting out should be begun about mid-March.

Potatoes are split into first early, second early and maincrop varieties. First and second earlies do not store very well but are ready four to eight weeks before the maincrop. Maincrop seed does not need to be sprouted before planting.

Mark the outside side position of the row of pots with the line, place the pot, complete with sleeve if using polythene, on the manure against the line, drop a seed into the centre of the pot and cover with 10 cm (4 in) of a compost mix, using 3 parts New Zealand bin compost, 1 part worm compost, 1 part Irish peat, 1 part perlite, 225 g (8 oz) of calcified seaweed, 110 g (4 oz) of rock phosphate, and 110 g (4 oz) of rock potash per 9-litre (2-gal) bucketful of mixed compost. Potatoes do not like alkaline conditions so do not add any dolomite or ground limestone.

Remove the sleeve for use in the next polythene pot, which is placed against the first pot, and so on along the row. By this method a row of potatoes is contained within 30 cm (12 in). If a second row is to be grown, butt this up against the first, but offset to fit the pots into the minimum space. The same applies to any additional rows. Fold over the top of the polythene to give protection, for the young growth is very tender and easily damaged by the slightest frost. As the foliage grows cover it again with 10 cm (4 in) of compost and continue doing so until the pot is completely filled. Water well during dry weather as the compost dries out very rapidly with the sides of the pot being exposed to the sun. I find it safer to water each container individually with the watering can rather than use a hose. Give each pot 9 litres (2 gal) each time to ensure the compost is thoroughly wetted.

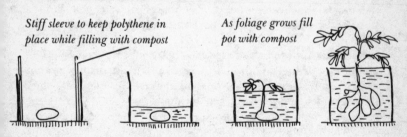

Stiff sleeve to keep polythene in place while filling with compost

As foliage grows fill pot with compost

GROWING POTATOES IN POLYTHENE POTS

As the pot-growing method is an attempt to get something for nothing in a small garden only earlier varieties should be considered to allow the land to be re-used when they have been harvested. Growing maincrop varieties will tie up the land until

October. I grow a first and second early to give a succession. To harvest, simply pull off the pot leaving the potatoes free to be lifted. There is no need for a fork; in fact lifting is so simple that if only half the quantity is required you can feel with your hand in the compost and lift out the number of potatoes you need, leaving the rest to carry on growing and stay fresh. I usually crop about 900 g (2 lb) per pot, but have had as much as 1.8 kg (4 lb) in a pot.

Should you have the space to grow potatoes conventionally, then draw out a trench about 15 cm (6 in) deep, apply the minerals as for the pot method and cover with 5 cm (2 in) of grass cuttings. Space the tubers 30 cm (12 in) apart for earlies and 38 cm (15 in) apart for the maincrop, then cover over with soil. Rows should be 60 cm (24 in) apart for all varieties. At the first signs of the shoots, start earthing up. At first draw only a little soil over from either side of the row and repeat every three to four days until a broad ridge has been formed with the shoots growing out of its apex. No further attention is required unless the weather is dry, when the trench between the rows can be filled with water. When harvesting, use a fork, not a spade, being as careful as possible not to damage the tubers – the object is to spike them with the table fork, not the garden fork!

Earlies are lifted when about the size of a hen's egg from mid-June onwards. Only lift as many as are required for a meal. These earlies do not keep well out of the ground and are spoilt even after a day or so.

Second earlies are ready by the end of July when the first earlies are finished. They can be stored, but in this case should be left in the ground until the skins are firm and cannot be scraped off by pressure with the thumb. The maincrop remains in the ground until the haulms have died back about the end of September, when they are lifted and prepared for storing.

RECOMMENDED VARIETIES
     First Early – Marius Bard
    Second Early – Wilja
        – Romano
      Maincrop – Majestic
        – Desiree

Radish

This is a very easy crop to grow and being very quick maturing, is excellent for successional cropping both in the greenhouse and outside. You can sow the seed in rows, very thinly 1 cm (½ in) deep, or broadcast over the ground, then cover it by running the rake back and forwards and crosswise to give about 5 mm (¼ in) of soil over the seed. They require no attention apart from watering in dry weather and can be lifted when large enough to use. Sown at two-week intervals from mid-March until the end of August, they will give a continuous supply over the season.

RECOMMENDED VARIETY   French Breakfast

Rhubarb

This is a valuable plant to have in the garden for its ability to produce a crop over a long period of time from a very limited space, and no garden should be without a root. It will fit very easily into an odd corner, but remember it has very large leaves which will smother anything within a 45 cm (18 in) radius.

The best way to start is to obtain a piece of root from the garden centre or the plant of a colleague in November or March. Make sure there is a good bud on the root. Plant it so that the top of the root is about 2.5 cm (1 in) below the ground level with any shoots still showing. The plants will stand for several years in the same spot, so the ground has to be well prepared with a dressing of 225 g (8 oz) per square metre (yard) of calcified seaweed followed with a 5 cm (2 in) layer of well-rotted compost.

Do not pull any sticks the first year after planting to allow the plants to develop fully and go gently in the second year. 'Pull' is the operative word for the sticks should not be cut or snapped off but gently pulled out of the crown. Remove any flower buds immediately they appear. Cropping should finish by the end of July.

Rhubarb can be forced to give an early crop from January onwards. In December selected crowns can be covered with large pots to exclude the light, then the pot covered with strawy manure to generate heat and increase the rate of growth. Stop pulling by the end of May when the pots should be removed and the plant left to recover for the next season.

Do not eat the leaves, which are poisonous, for they contain oxalic acid. However, this can be made to produce a very effective greenfly killer as described on page 144.

The number of plants is easily increased by splitting the root. Plants should be set out 75 cm (30 in) apart. Rhubarb can also be grown from seed. Sow during April in drills 2.5 cm (1 in) deep and thin out to 15 cm (6 in) between plants. Transplant to their permanent position in the autumn. As with the roots, do not pull the first year after planting out and limit the pulling during the second year.

RECOMMENDED VARIETIES   *Roots* – Hawke's Champagne
                            Seed – Holstein Bloodred

Spinach

Spinach has one big disadvantage in that it has a very short season and quickly runs to seed, especially if the weather is dry. To grow it successfully in the summer a number of small successional sowings need to be made. A sowing of the summer variety every two to three weeks from mid-March to the end of July with a single sowing of a winter variety in August and again in September will give an all-the-year-round crop.

Sow the seed 2 cm (¾ in) deep in rows 23 cm (9 in) apart, and thin out to 23 cm (9 in) between plants. Spinach does not like hot, dry positions so choose a moist, shady location. Prepare the ground three or four weeks before sowing with 225 g (8 oz) per square metre (yard) of calcified seaweed and as we are looking for those large green leaves, add blood, fish and bonemeal at 110 g (4 oz) per square metre (yard) followed by a 5 cm (2 in) mulch of well-rotted compost. Do not feed the winter variety, for too much lush growth will not withstand the cold winter weather. Do not allow the plants to dry out.

Start cutting as soon as the leaves are large enough to eat. Take only sufficient leaves for your needs, and leave the rest to carry on growing.

RECOMMENDED VARIETIES

    Summer – Longstanding
    Winter – Broad Leaved Prickly (it is the seed which
               is prickly not the leaves)

Spinach beet

Usually called leaf beet in the seed catalogues, for it is a variety of beetroot which is grown for its leaves and not for its roots. It is an excellent substitute for spinach, being easier to grow, one variety giving all the year round cropping. It is very hardy and even after being cut back by severe frosts will throw out new leaves in the spring. I grow it in the greenhouse to use purely as a winter crop.

For cropping all the year round, sow early in April and again at the end of July. Sow two seeds 2.5 cm (1 in) deep every 15 cm (6 in) in rows with 23 cm (9 in) between them or for greenhouse use, two seeds in an 8 cm (3 in) pot. Thin out the weakest seedling in either case. In the case of the pot sowing, transplant into the greenhouse soil as soon as the spring lettuces are finished.

Pick regularly to encourage the formation of fresh leaves. As with all perpetual crops, the more you pick the more it will produce. Allowing the leaves to grow old slows down the growth of fresh shoots.

RECOMMENDED VARIETY   Perpetual Spinach

Swedes

More popular in the north of the country, these are very hardy and will over-winter in the ground in even the severest of winters. They are very similar to the turnip, but I personally believe them to have a finer flavour.

Sow in May in rows 1 cm (½ in) deep, a pinch of seeds every 5 cm (2 in), with 38 to 45 cm (15 to 18 in) between rows. Thin out the seedlings to 15 cm (6 in) apart. Being a member of the brassica family swedes require the same pH levels (6.5 to 7.5) and precautions against club root disease. Harvesting can start from September right through to the following March. If they interfere with next year's cultivation, just lift and store them in a dry, airy place, leaving on as much root as possible. Cover the surrounding soil during frosty periods to enable a fork to be pushed into the ground for lifting.

RECOMMENDED VARIETY   Marian

Tomatoes

Although primarily regarded as a greenhouse plant, tomatoes can be grown very successfully outside if the correct weather conditions are available. In the small garden, however, the land is being used for so many other crops I feel there is no room for outside tomatoes, so I shall concentrate on the greenhouse crop. If you do not have a greenhouse a 25 cm (10 in) pot on a sunny window-sill will give very successful results. Many years ago, before I had a greenhouse, a south-facing shed window was sufficient to provide a plentiful supply of tomatoes for my family.

The seeds can be sown from mid-March in an 8 cm (3 in) plastic pot on the window-sill, in a temperature maintained at 18.5 to 21°c (65 to 70°F). When the seedlings are large enough to handle, prick out into individual pots, either the paper pots or if only one or two plants are wanted, into 8 cm (3 in) plastic pots. (Paper pots need to be in a block to retain their moisture and it is not desirable to mix the tomatoes with other seedlings.) Until a temperature above 10°c (50°F) can be guaranteed in the greenhouse keep the seedlings in the kitchen. Do not allow them to dry out at this stage and keep the plants growing. If the weather prevents planting out in the greenhouse, then transfer them to a larger pot at the first signs of the roots filling the smaller one.

Planting out will be some time in May when the minimum temperature can be guaranteed. If the odd cold night is forecast, for we can still have frost in May, then cover the tomatoes with a cloche or a large polythene bag for added protection. In my greenhouse they go into the same border as the carrots and beetroot, so if there is not a space then unfortunately some of these early roots will have to be lifted to accommodate the tomatoes. As the cucumbers will be grown on the north side in the same border, position a single row of tomatoes accordingly with 38 cm (15 in) between plants. Plant deeply, up to the seed leaves, and water well in after planting. The quantity of water will vary as growth proceeds, starting with about 285 ml (½ pint) per plant per day, increasing to 4.5 litres (1 gal) per plant when supporting full trusses of fruit. Water regularly, for more problems are caused through bad watering than any other cause. During the early stages, water each plant individually, and only apply a blanket cover to the border once the plants are supporting two trusses. Do not use the rose on the watering can. Always water directly out of the spout in order to soak the soil and not the foliage.

The plants will need to be supported when tall enough. Strings hung from the roof can be used in the wooden greenhouse where hooks can be screwed in. Let the string hang loose and wind the end of it two or three times round the stem. As the plant grows, continue to wind the string around the stem. Use a good size of hook to prevent the weight of the plant pulling it out of the roof. Once the stem has been bent over and creased, growth above this point will be retarded and the crop subsequently reduced.

In the aluminium type of greenhouse canes will have to be used. Push them well into the ground, for the weight of a plant carrying several trusses of fruit is sufficient to pull them over. Tie the plant loosely to the cane with a piece of soft string, making a figure of 8 to enable the tie to move with the plant and leaving room for the stem to swell. Place the canes in the hole before planting to avoid damaging the roots.

Growth is restricted to a single stem. Any side shoots which develop at the point where the leaf joins the stem should be removed, but take care not to break the skin of the stem. Stop the plant after the sixth truss by pinching out the growing tip. This not only restricts growth to the height of the roof, but directs the strength into producing six good trusses.

You can help the setting of the flowers by encouraging bees into the greenhouse to pollinate them or by artificial fertilisation using a camel-hair paintbrush (in my childhood the common implement

Pinch out side shoots between leaf stalk and main stem

DE-SHOOTING TOMATOES

was the tip of a rabbit's tail), or by tapping the supports gently from time to time to shake pollen into the atmosphere. Maintaining a little moisture in the atmosphere by pouring water on the path during a hot day or syringing the plants with a very fine spray also aids fertilisation. The first trusses suffer most of all from poor setting due to the limited number of flowers, so give these careful attention.

Feeding is very important and a boost will be needed as soon as the first fruits begin to swell. Apply calcified seaweed at a rate of 225 g (8 oz) per square metre (yard), and chopped comfrey leaves, followed by a 5 cm (2 in) thickness of half-rotted worm compost. A repeat dose three to four weeks later omitting the calcified seaweed and coupled with a foliar feed of comfrey liquid twice a week will give the plants the necessary feeding. I will crop an average of 5.7 kg (12½ lb) of fruit per plant and in one season I managed to average 6.8 kg (15 lb) per plant on this comfrey and worm compost feed.

The fruit requires sunlight to ripen and at the first sign of ripening remove the dying bottom leaves. Do not remove healthy leaves as is common practice in the commercial field; they are an integral part of the feeding system and must be left on for as long as they are healthy.

Removing the bottom leaves also aids ventilation, which is an important factor. Ventilate freely in hot weather, open the vents and the door. Too much heat will cause leaf scorching.

RECOMMENDED VARIETIES   Sweet 100
    Moneymaker
    Alicante

Turnips

Turnips are excellent for a successional crop. Starting from the end of May sow seed 1 cm (½ in) deep in rows when space becomes available and if sown thinly, any further thinning needed can take place when the roots are large enough to use. Start lifting when they are about golf-ball size, scrub and eat them raw in salads. Continue sowing as space becomes available until the end of July.

RECOMMENDED VARIETY   Golden Ball

Chapter Nine

Pests and diseases

Prevention is more effective than cure and throughout the seasons some of our efforts will be channelled towards this end. There is nothing more disheartening than a garden riddled with pests and disease, but in such cases the gardener deserves little sympathy because most of the trouble will be his own fault. By sticking to a few easy-to-follow basic principles, pests and disease can become a thing of the past, although I must admit there are one or two persistent pests which require on the spot attention.

Many of the problems encountered by the chemical user do not exist in the organically cultivated garden, for a natural balance is built up by nature between the pest, its predator and the environment. The organic gardener allows nature to tackle the enemy, only becoming involved when a helping hand is required. He does not try to take the job of control away from nature or supersede her methods; a policy of 'no interference' must be adopted. However, if assistance is required then this must be by using materials harmless to all but the pest. Even then it is better sometimes to discourage rather than kill.

Soil fertility

Healthy plants will only exist in healthy soil and healthy plants are more resistant to attack from pests and diseases. It is no figment of the imagination that organically grown plants are healthier, for their looks, smell and flavour are living proof. By applying organic matter and the well-balanced organic fertilisers, the soil becomes very fertile with a bountiful supply of nutrients and minerals to prevent the plants suffering from the deficiencies which leave them vulnerable to attack. Pests and disease are a sure indication of unhealthy soil.

In a previous chapter I have outlined the demands plants place upon the soil nutrients and how if incorrect feeding procedures are used then very quickly the soil can be deprived of its ability to meet the needs of the plants. Too generous an application can be just as damaging as a deficiency. The over-application of lime can lock up valuable nutrients making them unavailable to the plants. The over-application of nitrogenous fertilisers produces soft, lush growth which not only reduces yields, but leaves the plant susceptible to fungus disease attacks.

Following the instructions I have laid down for making compost, its use and the application of seaweed general fertilisers and foliar feeds will keep the soil rich and the plants producing healthy growth. The only time soil fertility will be a problem is during the transition period from chemical to organic cultivation. There is no instant formula to build up the required level overnight; it takes several years. During the first season the garden will be in an inbetween condition and the pests and diseases will take advantage of the situation if you allow them to. Do not be disheartened; the soil condition will improve as each year goes by and even as early as the second year the level of damage can be less than when chemicals were used for control. It will take anything up to seven years to clear the soil completely of chemical residues.

There are many organic-based remedies available to help you over these early years, but these take time and effort which can be more profitably used on other jobs, so the sooner the soil fertility is built up the better off you will be.

However, it is not possible to be totally immune at all times just by applying compost and organic fertilisers. Health does not appear to deter such pests as the carrot root fly, so precautions must be taken. For such occasions the Henry Doubleday booklet *Pest Control Without Poisons* is a valuable publication to have in your bookcase. I have heard that organic produce contains more protein than chemically grown crops, so that pests do not need to eat so much of it.

Soil sterilisation is not a practice I would recommend for it destroys – even though only temporarily – much of the good work being done by your feeding methods. As a result of the high temperature needed to kill pests and diseases the beneficial organisms in the soil also suffer, without any real guarantee that the soil has been effectively cleansed. Jack Temple has grown cabbages in the same greenhouse for twenty years, keeping the soil fertility high with a regular mulch of worm compost. This has proved very effective and the plants have been healthy and disease free throughout this time.

Garden hygiene

Keep it clean – three simple words but of the utmost importance if we are to succeed in a policy of prevention rather than cure. Everyone has a corner somewhere in the garden for storing canes, trays, boxes, pots and the other odds and ends which come in useful from time to time. Failing to keep this utility area clean is not only unsightly but also it can be a breeding ground for pests.

Set aside a specific area with a flagged or concrete base. This is so much easier to keep clean with a brush or hose than it would be if everything were sitting on the soil. Wash items before placing them in the corner; remember that disease can be transmitted in soil which is left clinging to them. A handy tool is a household dishwashing brush. I give everything a good scrub and if the dirt is a bit stubborn use a spot of detergent in warm water, rinsing well to remove any residue of suds. Do the cleansing as and when each item requires it. I find if they are left until there is a pile it becomes a chore.

I collect odd pieces of wood, old fence posts and planks which are ideal for holding the polythene down over the winter, the planks also serving as treading boards to save walking on the soil. Stack these on end; if they lie flat they become waterlogged and start to rot, making an ideal habitat for woodlice and millipedes.

The 'keep it clean' policy applies all over the vegetable garden. Do not leave rotting vegetation lying around; this is the way to attract slugs. Collect it up and put it in the compost bin. The same applies with roots; whenever a crop has been harvested, do not leave the roots in the ground (with the exception of the legume family with their nitrogen-fixing nodules), but lift the whole plant, cut off the head for use, shake the soil off the roots and add them to the compost. In the case of the brassica family, however, take the roots to the bonfire or the dusbin. *Do not* compost brassica roots in case you are spreading club root disease.

Keep the bottom of hedges and fences free from fallen leaves and weeds. Rubbish left in such places enables pests to survive the winter ready to attack the garden the following year. Pests and disease will attack weeds and many weeds are related to the vegetable families, so unless steps are taken to remove or suppress them, the weeds can offer a foothold for the pest to attack the crops. Quite often weeds will show the first signs of attack, so examine them when removing or suppressing and if the warning signs are there extend the examination to the vegetables.

The corners of the greenhouse are other areas to keep clean, particularly in the wooden type. The old dishwashing brush and water should be applied in the late autumn and again in early spring in case some pests eluded the autumn wash. These periods are also the times when the greenhouse is at its emptiest, so the corners are easy to get into. It is also a good time to wash the glass inside and out to ensure that the crops will get the maximum amount of light.

Do not leave old potatoes lying about; many potato diseases are passed on from infected tubers.

Diseased material

Most vegetable diseases are caused by fungi which can attack both the roots and the foliage. Often the symptoms are easily recognised, such as club root, or moulds or spots on the foliage. The virus diseases are more difficult to diagnose, but if a plant is misshapen or growing out of character to others of the same variety, then the odds are it is being attacked by a virus.

One of the requirements for good compost making is that the heap must be capable of developing temperatures high enough to sterilise diseased material. I am in full agreement with this statement, but for the small garden, I firmly believe diseased material should not be deliberately added to the compost heap. If for some unaccountable reason the high temperatures needed to kill off the disease are not reached, it is there waiting in the compost to be spread around the garden. The amount lost by destroying the diseased material is minimal and just not worth the risk.

Action must be taken immediately any trouble is noticed; to leave diseased material in the ground or lying around can result in the disease spreading to unaffected plants. Be careful when lifting not to leave pieces in the ground or drop any when removing them from the garden. Destroy by burning or putting them in the dustbin. To prevent any spreading of a disease I recommend that all diseased material is put into a polythene bag and the neck tied up before being dropped into the bin liner. The refuse is used to fill in quarries, and by the time the land is reclaimed the disease will have died off. Some councils incinerate all the refuse.

Wash your hands and tools after handling, and watch your feet; walking on diseased material or soil can also be dangerous.

Cultural precautions

Plants must be free from pests and diseases before planting, and the only way to safeguard this is to grow your own from seed, using your own composts which are known to be clean. It is all too easy in the case of the novice for infection to pass unnoticed, or it may be that the symptoms have not yet developed. To plant out unhealthy plants only passes the trouble over to unaffected plants and to the ground which can be infected for many years to come. I have already mentioned my experience with bought cabbage plants importing club root.

Diseases can be transmitted in seed, and the work carried out by the seedsmen on the disease testing of seed does greatly reduce the chances of this occurring. This can be one of the dangers of saving your own seed, for it is very difficult for the individual to safeguard against this source of infection, but you would be unlikely to buy a packet of infected seed from one of the reputable seed merchants. Potatoes, peas, French beans, celery and tomatoes are the plants most likely to be affected should this occur.

The seed merchants are also putting considerable resources into the breeding of immune or resistant strains of varieties which were previously vulnerable to attack. This is one of the reasons for the introduction of new varieties and the disappearance of the old. The seedsmen are not backward in advertising these facts in the catalogues and in some cases even list the lack of resistance to certain diseases. Good examples of this type of varietal resistance can be found in the lists of potatoes, French beans and lettuce. Choose an immune or resistant variety and play it safe.

The sowing of seed in conditions too wet or too cold for good germination renders the seed and seedlings liable to attack. Poor germination is more often the result of sowing under unfavourable conditions than of faulty seed. The plants must be kept growing and not checked by lack of water or poor soil conditions. Balanced feeding and a high organic content in the soil produces a good strong root system and a plant capable of fighting off attacks from pests and disease. The old favourite 'crop rotation' prevents the build up of disease in the soil. The most favourable growing conditions must be presented to the plants throughout their growth.

Predators – the gardener's friends

Let nature carry out the first assault using her powerful weapon, the pest's natural predators. This is where the organic gardener has an advantage over his chemical counterpart for his poison-free environment is a safe haven for insects and wild life who help to keep the pests at bay. It is all too easy to take their efforts for granted, for many of them work unseen, devouring the pests, giving us a clean, healthy crop. The list is too numerous to go into the details of every species, so I will only mention the more important ones. If you want more detail the book *Garden Pests and Predators* by Elfrida Savigear is well worth reading.

If in doubt about an insect in the garden, the old folk lore of 'if agile it is a friend and slow moving it is a foe' is as good a rule to work to as any. We are all too quick at getting out the spray and killing everything in sight, whereas if we only stood back for a few seconds and looked carefully at what was in front of us, then on many an occasion we would see that we were not alone in our fight against pests.

Birds

To many gardeners birds are only a nuisance, for they can do considerable damage. In the spring when the young pea shoots are just poking through the soil, or a row of young lettuce or cabbage plants has just been planted out, these can all be reduced to ground level in a matter of hours. Fruit trees and bushes are often damaged and we have to erect nets to give protection.

On the other hand, birds do far more good around the garden than they do damage. They eat all types of grubs, insects, slugs and caterpillars. To give an example of their benefit, this past season my garden was permanently full of cabbage white butterflies, more than I can ever remember seeing before and yet I had minimal damage to the brassica plants, and only hand picked no more than a dozen egg clusters or caterpillars. Every time I approached, flocks of birds rose from the plants. They were controlling the caterpillar population for me. You do not get very much in life free so in return for the good work done by the birds you must take precautions against damage and protect the most vulnerable plants.

Black beetles
The black beetles found under the polythene after mulching are friends – they are the ground beetle, feeding on eelworms and other larvae and insect eggs.

Centipedes
Often confused with the millipede but easily distinguished by their very much faster movement in the soil. Millipedes curl up into a ball when disturbed. The centipede feeds on small insects and slugs.

Frogs and toads
Although water is required for their breeding, both can live quite happily on land provided there is a source of food. Both should be encouraged into the garden for they are excellent controllers of slugs, woodlice and even mice, and are especially handy to have around the greenhouse, keeping down the slug population when the early lettuces are in the soil.

Hedgehogs
A friendly little creature and a great boon to the gardener, for he will eat a variety of insects, slugs, cutworms, woodlice and millipedes. If you find one in your garden then make an effort to persuade him to stay by providing a good supply of food, the traditional menu being a dish of bread soaked in milk. He may not want to live in the garden but if the food source is there he and his family will be quite happy to come and go, as they do in my own garden, returning each evening to dine and then back to their

shelter by the morning. You may not even know they've been but for the tell-tale droppings on the lawn next day.

Hoverfly
Very much like a small wasp with its black and yellow striped body, it can be recognised by its ability to hover in one position and then dart from one flower to another, just as its name implies. It is the larvae which are voracious feeders on aphids. They can be encouraged into the garden by planting yellow flowers: I find they are very much attracted to tagetes. The larvae are ugly little creatures, green-grey or brown with a pair of nippers to hold their prey.

Lacewings
A delicate-looking insect with either green or brown bodies and practically transparent wings. Their larvae also have a large appetite for aphids and other small-bodied insects. The larvae are very active and have a flattish, yellowy-brown body with a vicious pair of pincers. The eggs are laid in bunches on the underside of a leaf.

Ladybird
Familiar to gardeners with its red body and black spots, this insect and its larvae eat vast quantities of aphids. The larvae are not always recognised as friends as their slate grey colour does tend to lead many to number them amongst the pests. They are differentiated from a pest in that they are very much more agile.

Companion planting

It is well known that plants react to other plants growing around them, some growing very well together and others totally disliking their neighbour. The reason for this is that each plant has its own character, producing root excretions or odours either benefiting or repelling other species. These secretions and odours also have an influence on soil micro-organisms, and insects both soil and airborne. By careful selection, plants can give a very effective pest control. The growing of plants together for the benefit of other plants or to discourage pests is called 'companion planting'. Many of the old wives' tales have a great deal of truth in them and can be put to very good use especially in the greenhouse, where the conditions often favour such pests as whitefly and greenfly. Once colonies become established they are difficult to remove or even control, but the permanent guard of a deterrent plant prevents any attempted infestation ever being started.

The number of combinations is almost endless and could make up a book on their own. In fact a number of books have been written on the subject and are a valuable addition to the bookshelf.

Attacking the foe

Following the simple rules laid out earlier in this chapter will go a long way to avoiding problems in the garden, but we must be prepared for the odd occurrence of attack, and remedial action must be carried out. In these cases only the 'safe' poisons must be used. Do read the instructions carefully and use them accordingly. Take action at the first signs of attack. Do not let the pest or disease become established and spread around the garden, for then it may be too late. The strength of a pest is in its numbers and with their ability to breed at phenomenal speeds a few soon becomes a great many. Some of the 'safe' poisons do affect the friendly insects, so make sure use is restricted to the time of day which minimises damage to anything other than the pest. This applies to both home-made and proprietary organic mixtures. Spraying is best carried out in the late evening, by which time most of the friendly insects have settled down for the night. An hour before sunset is recognised as being the best time, for bees will have returned to the hive.

The choice between home-made and the proprietary mixture is one of personal choice. There should be no prejudice against the bought product simply for being on the same shelf as the chemical poisons. They are all manufactured from plant origins. Unless you have a bottle permanently in stock, then you will need to revert to the home-made remedy in the event of an emergency.

The home-made poisons are very easily produced, but remember, I do call them 'poisons', so treat them accordingly. Make them up in an old pan which is not used for cooking. Clean all equipment after use. Keep out of reach of children, and unless they are to be used immediately, bottle and label them clearly. These solutions do have a very limited shelf life, 24 hours at the most, so it is always safer to use them straight away.

For attacking aphids, rhubarb, elder, or wormwood leaves make very effective killers. The procedure is the same for all three, but only half the quantity of wormwood leaves is needed.

Chop up 450 g (1 lb) of leaves – 225 g (8 oz) for the wormwood –and add to 1.2 litres (2 pints) of water. Bring to the boil and simmer for half an hour. The water level in the pan will drop due to evaporation, so keep it topped up to the 1.2 litre (2 pint) level. Although the smell is not unpleasant, it does linger on for some time, so preferably this should be done on a camping stove outside, or in the garage or shed.

Strain the contents through an old pair of nylon stockings, muslin or sieve, if you have one, to remove the sludge. If you do not strain it, there will be a permanent battle keeping the spray nozzle clean. Further dilute it with 2.5 litres (4 pints) of water. The order of these actions can be reversed; it does mean you strain more liquid, but it is much cooler after being diluted with cold water. The rhubarb and elder solutions are both harmless to bees.

For caterpillars, particularly the cabbage white, a soapy water solution gives very good results. Any type of soap can be used, but the industrial soft soap is better, if you can get it. Simply dissolve 55 g (2 oz) of soap in 4.5 litres (1 gal) of hot water, and use when cool. Soapy water can also deter aphids if sprayed during the early stages of an attack.

The portions of these insecticides can be varied to give more or less solution as required.

Derris can be bought both in a liquid and a powder form for use against aphids, caterpillars, thrips and flea beetles. It is harmless to animals and birds, but unfortunately will kill bees, fish, the ladybird larvae and eggs, and the lacewing larvae. It remains toxic for a period of 48 hours after use, so must be used with care.

Pyrethrum has a toxicity period of only 12 hours, so can be safely used in the evening after the bees and ladybirds are out of the way and by morning its effects will have been neutralised. It is very effective as a fungicide and for general use against aphids.

Both these products can be obtained from any garden centre, but read the label on the pyrethrum bottle carefully. If you see the words 'Piperonyl butoxide' leave it alone, for this is not an organic product, but a chemical aphid killer added to the pyrethrum to produce a cheaper product. Buy only pure pyrethrum liquid.

Rotenone and quassia are also useful against aphids, caterpillars and other insects.

Common pests and diseases

Ants

These are not really pests, but they do have two damning features in that their burrowings loosen the soil around the plants, weakening the root structure and leaving the plant open to attack. They will also protect aphids from their predators for they 'farm' the aphids for their honeydew, the sweet, sticky substance excreted by the aphids. One form of control is to eliminate the aphids, but if ants do become a nuisance, then a mixture of equal parts of borax and icing sugar laid near the ants' runs and covered to protect it from the rain is the best method of control. Ants are sweet toothed, and the icing sugar is a very good disguise for the borax, which is poisonous to ants. As they eat their own excreta it does not take long for the borax to spread through the colony.

Aphids

This general heading includes the many species of blackfly, greenfly and whitefly, all of which damage the plants by sucking the sap, particularly attacking the young growing tips and seriously weakening the plants.

Blackfly is associated with the bean families. Some measure of control can be given by pinching out the growing shoot, particularly on broad beans, but for bad infestations, one of the products discussed previously must be used. Spray both sides of the leaves; aphids are very good at hiding and you will find just as many on the underside of the leaves as on the top.

Greenfly and whitefly in the greenhouse can be very troublesome. Breeding several times a week in the greenhouse environment, which is ideal for this purpose, it does not take long before the situation becomes out of control. Whitefly are particularly resistant and I find that many of the recommended sprays are totally ineffective. It is even resistant to undiluted Domestos, such is the persistence of this pest. However, all is not lost, for the most effective deterrent is achieved by companion planting. The planting of tagetes and nasturtiums in the greenhouse will keep control of the greenfly and whitefly. These are best planted early in the season before the pests appear, but if planted after the greenhouse has been invaded, it does not take long before their effects are noticed.

Choose a variety of tagetes with a strong smell – so many of the modern varieties have traded smell for looks. The variety I prefer is Signata Golden Gem (available from Unwin's). The choice of variety of nasturtium does not seem to be so important.

I do not limit the use of tagetes to the greenhouse. You can also edge the paths with it around the vegetable plot. Not only are they offering protection to the crops, but they also give great pleasure on a quiet summer's evening, filling the air with their fragrance.

The cabbage aphid is a real pest, for it penetrates into the heads of sprouts, cabbages and cauliflowers, making them unfit to eat. The sign of attack is that the leaves become yellow and begin to curl up and on examination masses of bluish-grey, mealy-looking aphids will be found on the underside. Leaves never really recover from the attack and in severe cases the plant will be stunted and even die, the effects being worse on young plants.

As with the whitefly, I find these aphids resistant to many of the sprays, the only effective one being nicotine. I have not discussed nicotine in the home-made insecticide sections, as it is not one I recommend using unless in an emergency, such as an attack by the cabbage aphids, for it is highly poisonous to humans, animals, birds and fish. Because of this use carefully, wash all equipment including your hands thoroughly after use, avoid contact on the skin and eyes, and keep well away from children and pets.

Making it up is simple; just add 55 g (2 oz) of cigarette ends, including filter tips, to 570 ml (1 pint) of water, boil for half an hour, then strain through a lady's old stocking. Dilute the concentrated solution with a further 2.5 litres (4 pints) of water; soapy water can be added for this helps the nicotine liquid to 'wet' the leaves. Spray both sides of the leaves, ensuring they are well soaked.

Blossom end rot
This is a disease which can cause heavy losses of the tomato crop. A small black spot appears on the bottom of the fruit, which grows larger with the fruit growth, and finally the end of the fruit becomes hard and flattened.

The cause is bad watering, allowing the plants to dry out. Quite often there is a delay between the period of dryness and the disease making an appearance. There is no cure. Affected fruit should be removed for secondary infections can start in them. Prevention depends upon regular and adequate watering throughout the growing period. Some recent studies have shown there is a link between blossom end rot and a calcium deficiency. Maintain calcium levels with an application of calcified seaweed, dolomite, or limestone.

Botrytis
This is sometimes known as 'grey mould' because of the fluffy greyish mould which appears on the affected plants. Needing cold, damp weather in order to get a foothold, it is at its worst in the autumn outside, and over the winter period and early spring in the greenhouse. Lettuces are particularly vulnerable to this disease, the stem rotting just above ground level.

Prevention is by not handling seedlings by their stems, but always by the seed leaves, and in the case of winter lettuces, do not plant too deeply and use varieties specifically for growing over winter. Tomatoes are also liable to attack, usually where leaves and side shoots have been removed. Take care not to break the skin when defoliating or side shooting. These should break off naturally at the joint without leaving any wound for the disease to enter.

Cabbage root fly
In April to early May the fly, very similar in appearance to a house fly, lays its eggs just under the surface next to the plant's stem. The eggs hatch out into little white maggots, which then attack the roots. The first sign of attack is when the leaves start to droop and turn a bluish colour, and when lifted it can be seen that the roots have been eaten away. Young plants damaged in this way very seldom survive.

The fly needs to lay its eggs in soil near the brassica roots, so the obvious solution is to prevent this by covering the soil immediately around the plant's stem. This can be done immediately on planting out. There are several methods. The most popular is to cut a small hole in a 10 cm (4 in) square of stiff weatherproof material (roofing felt or thick card will do), slit from the hole to one edge, then place it round the plant on top of the soil. Care is needed for it will keep off the rain. Alternatively, take an empty yogurt carton, make a hole in the bottom (easily done with a candle flame), slit the side with a pair of scissors, turn it upside-down and place it round the plant's stem, with the leaves through the hole. Hold the carton together by gently earthing up round the rim. Both these methods prevent the fly getting within reach of the soil where it needs to lay eggs.

However, the method I prefer is a combined protection with club root control, and consists of trenching out the row to about 10 to 15 cm (4 to 6 in) deep. Plant out the brassica plants and as they grow earth up with compost every week. Brassicas are very good at throwing out roots and will very quickly send new roots into the compost. If the root fly has attacked the plant, it takes about seven days for the eggs to hatch and the roots attacked will be the old ones, the new roots providing the plant with sufficient nutrients to survive the attack and produce a crop.

Carrot root fly

The first sign of attack is the foliage turning a maroon colour, and when lifted you can see small holes bored into the root. Cutting open the carrot exposes the little white maggots which have done all the damage. There is no cure; the only remedy left is to lift the attacked roots, cut off the damaged portions and use the remainder. Do not store with the maggots still inside, for they will carry on eating away and may even infect good roots. Affected roots do not store well anyway, tending to rot around the infected area.

The fly is attracted to the carrots in May and June, by smell. It lays its eggs on the surface of the soil ready for them to attack the roots when hatched. As you very rarely see the fly, it is not possible to attack it when laying its eggs. You only find out it has visited your crop when it is too late and there are the tell-tale signs on the leaves and in the roots. The only course open is to take precautions against the fly laying the eggs. There are many methods practised to minimise the carrot scent being signalled to the fly, sowing thinly for instance, to avoid having to thin out the rows, and if any thinning is required, this should be carried out on a still evening. Compost the thinnings, do not leave them lying about. However, as smell is the important factor, most of the precautions published rely on companion planting in an effort to disguise the smell. The suggestions are numerous, from mixing the seed with leeks, to grow a combined row of leek and carrot, to planting between rows of onions, or peas, or soaking string in paraffin and stretching it along the rows (but this taints the carrots). I have tried them all and have yet to find one to be 100 per cent successful.

However, there is one method which does give 100 per cent protection – completely covering the carrots with Papronet. Sow thinly, cover with the netting, either burying the edge in the soil or holding it down with bricks or wood so that no portion can be lifted off the ground by the wind to allow the fly to get in. There is no need to lift the netting till the crop is ready to harvest. The Papronet is porous enough to allow the rain through. When lifting, only remove sufficient net to lift what you need and then replace it immediately. There is a second wave of flies laying eggs in August and September. Carelessness then can ruin a whole season's efforts. There is a secondary benefit from the Papronet, as it acts as a cloche, giving weather protection in the early part of the season.

Caterpillars

The damage is caused by the larvae of the cabbage white butterflies and the other varieties of white butterflies and if left unchecked they can completely defoliate a plant in a short period of time. The eggs are laid in clusters on the leaves of the brassica family and are easily recognised by their bright yellow colour. They take about two weeks to hatch out, being fully grown in about four weeks. The spring and early summer brood will be butterflies by August, ready to lay eggs for a second attack on the plants.

The birds do a great deal in helping to control the levels, but you should still carry out regular checks to remove any remaining. Hand picking is the most effective; crush the eggs on the leaves and drop the caterpillars into a container. If laid out on the lawn, the birds soon finish them off. If hand picking is not to your liking, then one of the home-made or proprietary sprays will have to be used. At harvest time the safest remedy is to spray with 55 g (2 oz) of common salt in 4.5 litres (1 gal) of water. Remember to spray both sides of the leaves and do so at regular intervals, for the butterflies will be laying continuously.

Club root

This is the worst disease to affect the brassica family. Affected plants appear stunted and may even die off. The disease appears as swellings on the roots, which when cut open or left to decompose leave an obnoxious smell. The disease is caused by a fungus which can remain in the soil to re-infect plants in future years.

It is important therefore when lifting brassicas to use a fork and lift the whole root, making sure no pieces are left in the soil. Examine the root carefully for the tell-tale signs. *Do not* pull the root out by hand; this is a sure way of leaving sections of it in the soil. Lift the roots as soon as the cabbage, cauliflower, or the last Brussels sprout has been picked.

Club root can be imported by contaminated plants, soil, or manure. It is very contagious and every effort must be made to contain the disease and not to spread it around the garden. Drop the infected root, complete with soil, into a polythene bag. This prevents spillage of roots or soil on to clean parts of the garden, and you can destroy it either by burning it or putting it in the dustbin. *Do not compost*. Do not walk unnecessarily on infected soil, for any that sticks to your boots can transmit the disease.

Crop rotation is very important in the control of club root disease, as well as maintaining the correct pH level. Although club root will affect both acid and alkaline soils, the attack is not as damaging in alkaline soils, so it is important to hold the level as near to pH7 as possible. The only cure is time, but preventative action can be taken to grow brassicas successfully on infected ground.

To overcome the cabbage root fly I have described trenching out the row and as the plant grows, the trench is filled in with compost. By doing this the plant does not grow in the soil, but in the clean, uncontaminated compost, hence is not attacked by the club root. On infected soil, trench out deeper than for the root fly down to 20 or 23 cm (8 or 9 in), putting a layer of compost in the bottom before planting out, then earth up as the plant grows and you will produce healthy plants. If compost is scarce, then individual holes about 23 cm (9 in) square can be dug for each plant.

Slugs

These are probably the best known of all the pests and ones which can do considerable damage if left unchecked. Everyone is able to recognise the symptoms of attack, large parts of the leaves eaten away, plants keeled over having had the stem nibbled through at ground level, and the tell-tale slime trails. Unlike many of the other pests, you very seldom see slugs at work, for being nocturnal creatures they are not evident during daylight hours, and have retreated to their hideouts by the time we discover the damage. However, as they require a moist environment, if you go looking in the places which have been kept damp by a ground covering, rubbish at the bottom of the hedge, stones, pots or boxes left on the soil, there you will find them. The slug problem is more serious in wet weather, but in the driest of summers the hiding places previously mentioned do offer sufficient protection for the slug still to be a pest. Hygiene plays an important role in slug control. Discarded leaves and plants left to rot on the ground are the ideal menu for slugs, so do not leave rubbish lying around. Unfortunately this can work against you, for they prefer to eat semi-rotting material, and if you remove it all through good housekeeping practice, then the slugs will transfer their attentions to the next best, the growing plants. Not to worry, for by adopting the grass-cutting mulching techniques you have given the slugs what they want and they tend not to wander off to attack the crops.

If you feel the slugs are in sufficient numbers to need further attention, then there are several methods to trap or deter them. Lifting the newspaper and grass-cutting mulch will expose the slugs gathered there for collection and disposal. As night workers, a torchlight search party can be arranged to cover the garden area and remove the slugs, but the commonest method of control is the beer treatment. Sink a wide-mouthed shallow container into the ground so that the rim is level with the soil and fill it with a mixture of equal parts of beer and water, sweetened with sugar. Use a glass or glazed container, for the surface of plastic is sufficiently rough to enable the slug to climb out. Place these traps around the garden.

The slug is attracted to the mixture, falls in, and being unable to crawl out, drowns. Empty the containers, refill and replace in the ground.

For individual plant protection, especially in the greenhouse, I find the deterrent more effective. Slugs have a soft underbelly and do not like crawling over sharp materials, a sprinkling of which around the base of the plants gives very effective protection. Ashes or sharp sand can be used, but I much prefer crushed egg shells. When the oven is cooling down after a baking session, pop in a tray of egg shells. The baked shells can be crushed down in the hand and scattered on the soil around the plants. Egg shells have the added benefit of being not only free, but also a good source of calcium.

For plants outside, the eggshells are not as effective, for when wet they lie flat, cling together and offer no defence against the slug. I find paper pots offer individual protection outside. Leave about 1 cm (½ in) of the pot above soil level. When the paper dries out it leaves a sharp edge which the slug will not crawl over. Even in rainy weather the paper stays dry, protected by the leaves of the plant.

Don't forget the natural enemies of the slugs, especially the birds and hedgehogs. They are on your side.

Potato diseases

The diseases associated with potatoes are many and the subject of a book on their own. By using calcified seed and selecting immune varieties, the problems for the amateur gardener are reduced to one or two.

Common scab

Probably the commonest complaint with potatoes, but fortunately this is not a serious disease. The unsightly markings cause wastage because of the necessity to peel the potatoes, but that is about all. The scab is at its worst in alkaline soils lacking in humus and in hot, dry summers.

The cure is therefore simple: keep lime away from the potato plot, build up the humus level by adding plenty of organic matter, do not allow the soil to dry out, and select a variety showing resistance to attack. Grass cuttings added to the bottom of the potato trench is an added precaution in soil lacking in humus until a good level can be built up.

Blight

This is the worst of the diseases we will encounter and was the cause of the potato famine in Ireland in the 1840s. Early potatoes usually mature before blight comes on the scene so the disease is limited to the main crop. The first signs are the dark, discoloured areas on the leaves, which will turn to dark brown to black with a white mould on the underside of the leaves in the area of discoloration. This mould carries the spores of the disease which are responsible for it spreading to other plants. The foliage eventually dies, which stops any further growth of the tuber, giving a very much reduced yield. The tubers can also show signs of the attack with slightly sunken areas in which, when cut, a reddish brown rot can be seen beneath the skin.

Weather plays an important part, the disease being at its worst in warm, wet summers. Hot, dry weather can kill off the disease if it is restricted to the leaf only, but once it has reached the stem it will have no effect.

Prevention is always better than cure. Grow one of the many varieties which are blight resistant. Should you suffer an attack the only cure is to cut off the foliage and destroy it, putting it in a plastic bag so as not to spread the spores around the garden. Lift the crop and remove any damaged tubers and store in a sack separately from any other potatoes. Examine the tubers two weeks later, again looking for any signs of soft spots or rot, and repeat every two weeks. One rotting potato will soon spread the rot to others if left in storage for too long.

Do not leave any potatoes in the ground when lifting, for any infected tubers left to overwinter in the ground are a source of infection the following year. If the whole crop is affected, spray the foliage with a Burgundy mixture to kill off the fungi.

The Ministry of Agriculture issues a number of free leaflets covering pests and diseases. Though many of the controls advised are chemical the leaflets are worth having, for if nothing else, they help you recognise the pest, or the symptoms of the disease.

Useful information

Further reading

Organic Gardening – Lawrence D. Hills – PENGUIN BOOKS
Fertility Gardening – Lawrence D. Hills – CAMERON & TAYLEUR
Companion Plants – Philbrick and Gregg – WATKINS
Carrots Love Tomatoes – Louise Riotte – THORSENS
Garden Pests and Predators – Elfrida Savigear – THORSENS
Here's Health Magazine – Jack Temple's articles
Miscellaneous Leaflets – Henry Doubleday Research Association
MAFF Publications – Lion House, Willowburn Estate, Alnwick, Northumberland NE66 2PF
Worm Compost – Jack Temple – SOIL ASSOCIATION

Addresses

Organic Associations

Henry Doubleday Research Association, Convent Lane, Bocking, Braintree, Essex CM7 6RW

Soil Association Ltd, Walnut Tree Manor, Haughley, Stowmarket, Suffolk IP14 3RS

I recommend joining these Associations. Their aim is to promote organic horticulture and agriculture respectively. The membership fee is very modest for the services offered.

Many of the products I mention are available from garden centres but should you have any difficulty further information can be obtained from the following firms:

Fertilisers

Calcified Seaweed	Vitaseamin (S.C.) Ltd, Woodside, Charney Road, Grange-Over-Sands, Cumbria LA11 6BP
Seaweed Meal	Maxicrop International Ltd, 21 London Road, Great Shelford, Cambridge CB2 5DF
Alginure	Alginure Products Ltd, Bells Yew Green, Tunbridge Wells, Kent TN3 9BT

'Back to Nature'   P.B.I. Ltd, Britannica House, Waltham Cross, Herts

Clavering Products   The Real Garden Advisory Bureau, 36 The Green, Woburn Green, Bucks HP10 0EU

Miscellaneous products

Black Polythene Sheeting (500 gauge)   Weldbank Plastic Co. Ltd, Devonshire Road, Chorley, Lancs PR7 2BY

Temple System   Newman Turner Publications Ltd, Unit 18, Goldsworth Trading Estate, Woking, Surrey

Papronet   Papropac Ltd, Wyke Works, Hedon Road, Hull HU9 5NL

A. P. Propapack Polystyrene Trays   Samuel Dobie & Son Ltd

Ambig Seed Raiser & Sprouter   Newman Turner Publications Ltd

Rotol Compost Bin   Lindvale Plastics Ltd, Waverley Street, Coatbridge, Lanarkshire

Compostabin   Garotta Products Ltd, Station Mills, Bute Street, Luton, Beds LU1 2HE

Perlite   Silvaperl Products Ltd, P. O. Box 8, Dept 38, Harrogate, North Yorkshire HG2 8JW

Soil Testing Kits   J. Arthur Bower, Horticultural Advisory Service, Wigford House, Lincoln LN5 7BL

Seeds

Catalogues for mail orders can be obtained from the following:

Unwins Seeds Ltd, Histon, Cambridge

Samuel Dobie & Son Ltd, Upper Dee Mills, Llangollen, Clwyd

J. W. Boyce, 67 Station Road, Soham, Ely Cambridgeshire CB7 5ED

Chase Seeds Ltd (organically grown), Gibraltar House, Shepperton, Middlesex TW17 8AQ

Asmer Garden Shop Ltd, 144 Priorwood Road, Taunton, Somerset

W. W. Johnson & Son Ltd, Boston, Lincs.

Index

oxygen 16, 22, 36, 39

Papronet 58, 59, 68, 69, 79, 87, 98, 100, 105, 109, 110, 111, 149
parsley 116
parsnip 71, 80, 83, 123
peas 59, 65, 79, 82, 83, 92, 123–6, 125d, 139, 149
peat 31, 32, 35, 50, 72, 127; pots 76
perlite 32, 47, 127
pesticides 12–4, 17, 47, 144
pests 13, 42, 56, 58, 60, 135–152; in greenhouse 85, 88
pH 31, 43, 47, 48–52, 66, 104, 131, 150
phosphate 17, 43, 46, 47; rock 46, 127
phosphorus 16, 30, 40, 45, 48, 93
pigeons 106
plan, cropping 55, 54d
planting out 29, 57, 77, 105d, 113, 119, 120, 126, 132, 151
poisons 11, 13, 143
pollution 18, 48, 66
polythene: bags 23, 32, 42, 72, 92, 132, 139, 150; cloches 68; sacks 24, 81; sheets 25, 27, 29, 36, 38, 39, 104, 126
polystyrene slabs 77, 111
potash 33, 41, 45, 47, 107; rock 46, 127
potassium 16, 30, 40, 43, 45, 46, 48, 93
potato 35, 59, 61, 65, 79, 81, 88, 126–8, 127d; diseases 49, 138, 139, 152–3
pots 56, 71, 72, 94, 104, 108, 129, 132; growing potatoes in 126; paper 8, 64, 74–6, 75d, 77, 99, 100, 101, 103, 104, 108, 110, 120, 122, 132, 152
potting compost 32, 35, 47, 46, 94
predators 11, 135, 140
press, comfrey 33, 34d

Propapack 77, 111, 119, 122
protein 16, 30, 31, 33, 43, 93, 136
putrefaction 21, 24, 33, 41
pyrethrum 144

quassia 145

radish 60, 62, 83, 90, 129
red spider mite 103
rhubarb 129, 144
ripening 45
rock: phosphate 46, 127; potash 46, 127
root fly, cabbage 104, 147–8, 150; carrot 109, 148–9
roots 16, 42, 44, 45, 46, 72, 77, 79, 113, 123, 124, 137, 148, 150
rosemary 116
rot 153; blossom end 45, 147
rotation, crop 10, 37, 55, 59, 60–3, 88, 140, 150
rotenone 145
Rotol bin 23, 27, 30, 32, 41; system 38

sage 117
salt 41, 150
salts, mineral 16
savoy 104, 108
scab 49, 152
scorching 17
Seagold 42–3
seaweed 18, 27, 40, 41, 42, 43, 44, 99, 100, 136; calcified 24, 31, 32, 38, 42–3, 51, 79, 105, 109, 111, 112, 114, 122, 123, 124, 127, 129, 130, 134, 147; meal 39, 43–4, 104, 122, 126
seeds 30, 45, 55, 56, 139; keeping 81–3; sowing 56, 57, 71–2, 77–9, 99, 109; sowing mixture 32, 35; sprouting 58, 90–3
seedtrays 68, 71, 76
sets, onion 122
sideshooting see de-shooting